D0559106

San Francisco Peninsula Bike Trails

32 Road and Mountain Bicycle Rides
through San Francisco and San Mateo Counties

by
Conrad J. Boisvert

Penngrove Publication
P.O. Box 798
Pescadero, CA 94060
www.penngrovepublications.com

For Sabrina, Matthew and Leila

Library of Congress Control Number: 2003098687
International Standard Book Number: 0-9621694-9-8

Cover photograph by Conrad Boisvert
Taken along Alpine Road
Cyclists: Kristi Webb and Paul McKowan

Photographs in the book were taken by Conrad Boisvert

Printed in the United States of America

First printing, November 1991
Second printing, September 1993
Third printing, May 2001
Second Edition, September 2004

℘enngrove Publications
P.O. Box 798
Pescadero, CA 94060
www.penngrovepublications.com

TABLE OF CONTENTS

ACKNOWLEDGMENTS

My sincere thanks goes out to all the cycling partners I have had over the years who have had the patience to deal with me and the many exploratory routes I have been inclined to try. I especially appreciate their patience with me, as together we conquered many hills that we sometimes expected and other times were surprised and maybe a little dismayed by. I hope they forgive me for the many unexpected roads or trails we followed and the frequent "extra options" we rode as together we learned the routes and found out the hard way the best routes to follow.

Much appreciation goes to Kristi Webb of the Midpeninsula Open Space District and to the many district park rangers who have always been very helpful and informative. The rangers and volunteers of the county and state park systems also deserve thanks for the fabulous work they do on an ongoing basis.

Bonnie Reyling deserves special mention for putting up with my idiosyncrasies and for making my life more wonderful than I thought possible. Thanks also to my terrific children, Judie, Charles, and Steve, for their ongoing moral support and encouragement.

Finally, this book would have been much more difficult to complete without the ongoing support, encouragement, and prodding of my publisher, Phyllis Neumann. Without her, I can only wonder whether I would have written the book or not. For this, I am exceedingly grateful.

EXPLORE THE PENINSULA BY BIKE!

Blessed with a near-perfect climate, a wide variety of terrain, spectacular natural beauty, and close proximity to the Pacific Ocean and San Francisco Bay, the San Francisco Peninsula is a cyclist's paradise. Few places can compare with the peninsula for the wealth of enjoyment and challenge available along the many country roads and mountain trails here, all within a short drive from nearly any population center.

Stretching from San Francisco in the north to Mountain View in the south and from the bay in the east to the ocean in the west, the San Francisco Peninsula is home to flatlands in the Santa Clara Valley, redwood forests in the coastal mountains, and the rugged coastline so characteristic of northern California. The large population of the peninsula and the ever-increasing popularity of recreational cycling have combined to fuel the search for the best roads and trails for riding.

Although there are plenty of pleasurable rides directly within the population centers on the peninsula, even better ones can be found on short trips to the surrounding countryside. Traveling along remote rural roads with little or no car traffic, cyclists are rewarded with the true pleasure of the outdoors and with natural scenery as varied as any in the entire country. The wooded foothills around Woodside and the remote country roads along the coast are examples of the outstanding cycling experiences accessible on the peninsula. World-class cyclists have been known to use the roads through the hills of the Santa Cruz Mountains as training grounds for international competition.

Mountain biking opportunities abound, as well, especially with the ongoing land purchases of the Midpeninsula Regional Open Space District. Even with convenient parking areas, well-prepared trail maps and plentiful trail signs, open space preserves still remain relatively undeveloped in order to allow their full enjoyment with minimal impact on their natural state. Mountain bikers, hikers, and equestrians share the trails within the preserves. County and state parks, while usually more developed than open space preserves, also offer spectacular scenery and enjoyment and often have educational and informative displays at each park headquarters.

The rides in *San Francisco Peninsula Bike Trails* have been carefully chosen to appeal to recreational cyclists of all abilities. There are assorted easy rides for the beginner, intermediate rides for those with a little more energy, and difficult rides for those looking for the challenge and rewards of bigger hills and longer distances. In all cases, the routes have been selected to provide the best scenery and the most safety. Don't hesitate — get on your bike and enjoy the beauty of the spectacular San Francisco Peninsula!

REGIONS ON THE SAN FRANCISCO PENINSULA

San Francisco and the Upper Peninsula

The northern part of the San Francisco Peninsula is dominated by the city of San Francisco and its spectacular bay. Golden Gate Park, in a class with any of the world's finest urban parks, offers a wide array of diversions, including art and natural history museums, the Steinhart Aquarium, arboretums, and numerous lakes and sport fields. Cycling along the shoreline of the bay and the ocean offers both inspiring views and many cultural and historical points of interest.

Woodside and the Mid-Peninsula

Nestled in the foothills of the Santa Cruz Mountains, the town of Woodside serves as a focal point for local cyclists and for those who have come from other places to ride here. Easily one of the most popular cycling areas in all of northern California, Woodside offers numerous country roads with a wide variety of terrain, ranging from flat and gently rolling, to climbs sufficient to challenge the most advanced riders. Recreational cyclists and top-level racing teams can commonly be seen sharing the roads on most weekends as they cruise past the many horse ranches and through the lush forests so typical of this region.

Palo Alto and the Lower Peninsula

Palo Alto, the home of Stanford University and the cradle of the high-tech revolution which spawned "Silicon Valley", is another cycling hotbed for the urban and suburban dwellers living in and around this region. Palo Alto was, in fact, one of the first cities to recognize the value of bicycle transportation and to establish an extensive network of bike lanes along local streets. Through pleasant residential neighborhoods and the architecturally fascinating Stanford University campus, and along the many peaceful country roads in the foothills, cyclists can experience relative remoteness, even when in close proximity to the population centers of the valley.

Along the Pacific Coast and on the Western Slope

In stark contrast to the regions of the Santa Clara Valley just over the mountains, the coast enjoys its own microclimate and has its own unique blend of country roads and trails. On summer days when the valley may be sweltering, the coastal region is often covered with a marine layer and blessed with temperatures considerably lower. In the winter, the temperature shift is often reversed, with the coast enjoying warmer temperatures than the inland regions. Farms, ranches, and forests dominate the landscape away from the shoreline and car traffic along inland roads on the coast is usually minimal.

THE SAN FRANCISCO PENINSULA

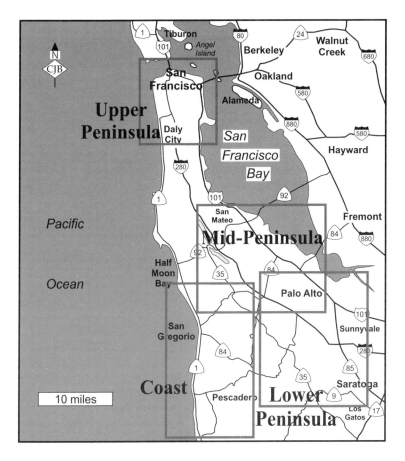

HOW TO USE THIS BOOK

Understanding the Ride Parameters

At the beginning of each ride description is a short list of ride parameters. These are intended to give you a brief summary of that particular ride and to permit you to quickly select the ride that most suits what you are looking for.

Ride Rating — Reflects the overall difficulty of the ride, a simple judgment that classifies it into one of three categories: *Easy*, *Moderate*, or *Difficult*. The rating results from an evaluation of both the distance and elevation gain for the ride and is also influenced by the steepness of the hills.

Distance — Indicates the length of the ride, excluding any optional side trips that might be included in the ride description.

Riding Time — Gives an indication of how much time to allow for the ride. Keep in mind however, that this does not include extended stops for sightseeing, eating, or rests. The riding time usually assumes a moderate pace of about 8-10 miles an hour for most types of terrain and a slower pace for harder rides.

Elevation Gain — Combines the total elevation gain for all the hills along the route.

Type of Bike — Suggests either road or mountain bike, depending on the route. Although a ride may have a stretch along a dirt section, it still may be suitable for a road bike, if it is smooth and safe.

Skill Level — Refers to the level of technical skills that a mountain bike ride requires. Skill levels are designated as *Non-technical*, *Somewhat technical* and *Very technical*. Rides with a *Non-technical* skill level usually have wide and smooth trails and modest grades along the climbs and descents. Those which require *Very technical* skills can have narrow trails with steep and bumpy conditions and may also have tight switchbacks to contend with.

About the Ride

This section outlines a general description of the ride along with any interesting background or historical information about the area. The route to be followed is explained, although the details are covered more fully in the *Ride Details and Mile Markers* section. Extra side trip or ride variations are sometimes outlined in order to enhance the ride. The nature of the terrain and the traffic to be encountered is also outlined.

Starting Point

The exact place to start the ride is described, along with detailed directions explaining how to get there. In general, rides are started at locations where free parking is readily available and where refreshments can be obtained. Typically the starting points are also easily recognizable places, simplifying the situation for a group of people meeting to ride together. On maps, the starting points are indicated with an asterisk. ✱

Elevation Profile

The elevation profile provides a detailed view of the hills along the route. It not only previews the climbing for you before you do the ride, but can be useful on the ride to help you anticipate the terrain ahead of you. Grades (in percent) for significant hill climbs are often indicated. A 10% grade is one that has about 500 vertical feet of elevation gain for each mile of distance.

Map

Each ride has a map associated with it indicating the route. Rides with more than one route are indicated with direction arrows for each route.

Ride Details and Mile Markers

Directions for the route are described along with elapsed distances. You don't necessarily need a cycle computer for following the route, since the markers come at frequent intervals and you will quickly learn to estimate distances accurately enough. The required turns to take are clearly indicated. Special sights or points of interest along the way are also indicated.

Shoreline Park in Mountainview

San Francisco
and the Upper Peninsula

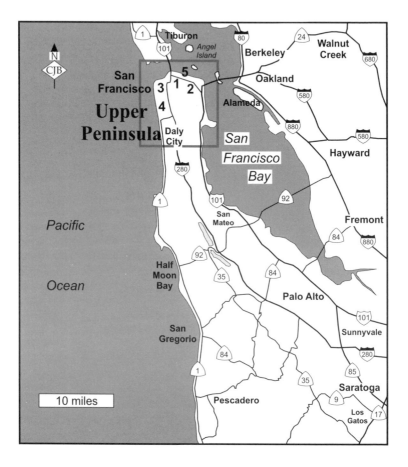

1 San Francisco

San Francisco to Tiburon with Ferry Return

Region: *Upper Peninsula*	**Distance:** *22 miles*
Ride Rating: *Easy*	**Elevation Gain:** *400 feet*
Type of Bike: *Road Bike*	**Riding Time:** *2-3 hours*

About the Ride

Stunning views of San Francisco and the Bay and an exhilarating boat cruise on the Blue & Gold Fleet ferry highlight this delightful ride. Starting from the Marina Green, the route leads along the waterfront and into the Presidio to the Golden Gate Bridge. Once across the bridge, the route follows surface roads into charming Sausalito. Continuing through Sausalito, you will then follow along a paved bike path that leads past the bay shoreline. More surface roads lead around Strawberry Point to another bike path to Belvedere and then finally to Tiburon.

In Tiburon, you can simply reverse the route to return on bicycle, or you can catch the ferry back to the city. The ferry will take you from Tiburon past Angel Island and Alcatraz and will deposit you at Fisherman's Wharf, from where you will return to the Marina Green along roads once again.

The ride is quite flat, except for some small hills in the Presidio and going over the Golden Gate Bridge and then another steep, but short climb just before Tiburon. While car traffic will be encountered on the roads, much of the route follows along paved multi-use trails.

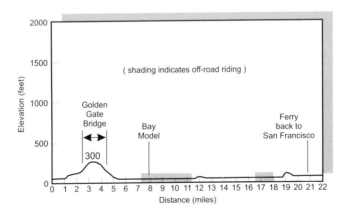

Starting Point

Begin the ride at the Marina Green, located between Fort Mason and the San Francisco Yacht Harbor. To get there, take the Civic Center exit off Highway 101 and follow Van Ness Avenue to Fisherman's Wharf and Aquatic Park. Turn LEFT on Bay Street, right on Laguna Street, and then left on Marina Boulevard. The Marina Green is on the right side. Public parking and restrooms are available.

Mile Markers

0.0 Proceed WEST along the bike path which follows Marina Boulevard.

0.7 Continue STRAIGHT to enter Crissy Field.

1.1 Turn LEFT onto Halleck Street.

1.3 Turn RIGHT onto Lincoln Boulevard and then bear RIGHT to stay on Lincoln Boulevard.

2.4 Just before you get to the bridge, turn RIGHT into the main visitor area. Look for the bike route to take you across the bridge. You cross over on either the east side (for weekdays) or the west side (for weekends).

4.7 Turn RIGHT onto Alexander Avenue at the north side of the bridge.

6.1 Turn RIGHT onto Second Street toward Sausalito.

6.3 Turn RIGHT onto Richardson Street and then LEFT onto Bridgeway Road along the waterfront.

7.2 After passing through central Sausalito, continue along the bike path on the right side of the roadway.

7. Bike path diverges from the road side — this is easy to miss.

7.9 Bay Model on the right side — scale model of the entire bay.

8.1 Turn LEFT to follow the road.

8.4 Turn LEFT on Harbor Drive and once again get on the bike path as it follows along Bridgeway Road.

11.3 At the end of the bike path, turn RIGHT onto East Blithedale Avenue.

12.2 After crossing over the freeway, turn RIGHT and follow the frontage road.

13.0 Turn LEFT onto Ricardo Road and then RIGHT onto Strawberry Drive. Follow this road all the way around and back to Tiburon Boulevard.

15.6 Turn RIGHT onto Tiburon Boulevard.

15.8 Turn RIGHT onto Greenwood Cove Drive.

16.5 Continue STRAIGHT at the end of Greenwood Cove Drive onto the paved bike path which leads along the shoreline.

18.0 Turn RIGHT onto San Rafael Avenue and then continue around Belvedere on West Shore Drive.

18.9 Climb the steep but short hill and continue along Beach Road.

20.6 Turn RIGHT onto Main Street into Tiburon.

20.8 The Blue & Gold Fleet dock is on the right side of Main Street, at the intersection with Tiburon Boulevard. Tickets are purchased on board. The ferry will take you to Pier 41 at Fisherman's Wharf in San Francisco where you will continue the ride. At Fisherman's Wharf, turn RIGHT onto Jefferson Street.

21.1 Turn LEFT onto Hyde Street and climb the short hill and turn RIGHT onto Beach Street.

21.3 Turn LEFT onto Polk Street and then RIGHT onto North Point Street.

21.5 Turn LEFT onto Van Ness Avenue and then RIGHT onto Bay Street — Fort Mason is on the right side.

21.8 Turn RIGHT onto Laguna Street and continue around Fort Mason and then turn LEFT onto Marina Boulevard.

22.0 End of the ride back at the Marina Green.

At the Harbor in Tiburon

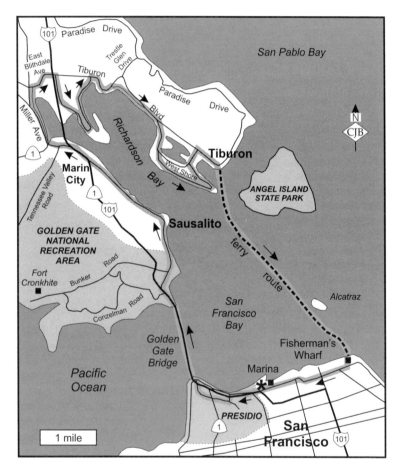

Ride No. 1

2   San Francisco
San Francisco Waterfront and the Presidio

Region: *Upper Peninsula*	**Distance:** *25 miles*
Ride Rating: *Moderate*	**Elevation Gain:** *1600 feet*
Type of Bike: *Road Bike*	**Riding Time:** *3 hours*

About the Ride

In 1776, about the time that the Declaration of Independence was being prepared and presented to the world a continent away in Philadelphia, the Spanish were making their presence felt in what is today San Francisco. Soldiers and missionaries arrived there to establish a settlement just south of the Golden Gate, greatly and irrevocably disrupting the lives of the Ohlone Indians living there at that time. The Presidio became a military base and stayed that way under Spain, Mexico, and finally, the United States. Playing some kind of role in all of the military campaigns in which the United States was involved, the Presidio was a picture of consistency as the city of San Francisco grew dramatically just outside its boundaries. Today, the Presidio is no longer a military base, but is instead a part of the larger Golden Gate National Recreation Area. Visitors can explore over 500 historic buildings located within the Presidio, as well as a national cemetery, numerous fortifications, and an old airstrip at Crissy Field.

The route of this ride begins along the Great Highway at Golden Gate Park. It initially follows along the Great Highway past the historic Cliff House and then leads into Lincoln Park and the California Palace of the Legion of Honor. After passing through the Presidio, the route then follows along the shoreline and passes the Marina Green, Fort Mason, Fisherman's Wharf, and the deep water piers, finally ending at the ballpark for the S.F. Giants baseball team. The return is along the same route.

There are several small hills along the way, but none are particularly difficult.

Starting Point

Start the ride at the western end of the park at the corner of the Great Highway and John F. Kennedy Drive, near the Murphy Windmill. Get there by way of 19th Avenue by turning off at the 25th Avenue exit and proceeding through the park to the west end at the ocean.

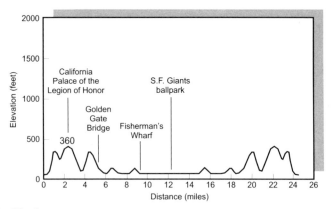

Mile Markers

0.0 Proceed NORTH along the Great Highway.

0.6 Cliff House on the left side.

0.9 Turn LEFT onto El Camino Del Mar and then RIGHT onto Seal Rock Drive.

1.3 Begin Clement Street.

1.7 Turn LEFT onto Legion of Honor Drive.

2.2 California Palace of the Legion of Honor on the left side.

3.1 Begin Lincoln Boulevard.

4.7 Pass under the approach to the Golden Gate Bridge.

6.5 Turn LEFT onto Halleck Street.

6.9 Turn RIGHT onto Mason Street in Crissy Field.

7.3 Continue STRAIGHT to follow the bike path which runs parallel to Marina Boulevard next to the sidewalk.

8.2 Turn RIGHT onto Laguna Street and then LEFT onto Bay Street.

8.7 Turn LEFT onto Van Ness Avenue and then RIGHT onto North Point Street.

8.9 Turn LEFT onto Polk Street and then RIGHT onto Beach Street.

9.1 Turn LEFT onto Hyde Street and then RIGHT onto Jefferson Street.

9.6 Bear RIGHT onto The Embarcadero. Look for bike lanes or ride on the sidewalk for safety.

12.2 End of the route at the ballpark — return back the way you came.

24.4 End of the ride back at Golden Gate Park.

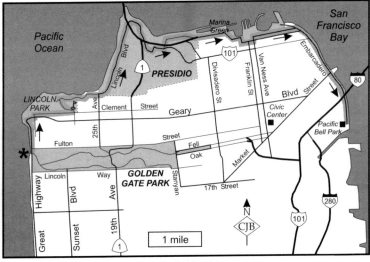

Ride No. 2

View of the Golden Gate Bridge from Lincoln Park

3　San Francisco
Tour of Golden Gate Park

Region: *Upper Peninsula*	**Distance:** *12 miles*
Ride Rating: *Easy*	**Elevation Gain:** *200 feet*
Type of Bike: *Road Bike*	**Riding Time:** *2-3 hours*

About the Ride

Golden Gate Park serves as a superb example of what an urban park can be. Reclaimed from barren land dominated by scrub oak and sand dunes, the park was constructed beginning in 1870. The addition of topsoil and the planting of a wide variety of plants and trees began the conversion of the land into what today serves as the centerpiece of the *San Francisco Recreation and Park Department* system.

Encompassing an area about three miles long and ½-mile wide, it contains the M.H. de Young Museum, the Asian Art Museum, and the California Academy of Sciences. In addition, the Japanese Tea Garden, Conservatory of Flowers, Strybing Arboretum and the Botanical Gardens add a natural flavor to the man-made efforts displayed in the museums. Scattered around the park are numerous lakes, meadows and pathways for relaxing and reflecting.

Spreckels Lakes is the home of the San Francisco Model Yacht Club and it is not unusual to find the lake occupied by miniature versions of classic racing boats. Paddle boats and rowboats can be rented at Stow Lake and free outdoor concerts are often performed on Sunday afternoons in the Music Concourse.

This ride takes you on a casual tour around the park, passing by nearly all of the major attractions. Be sure to bring a bike lock and be prepared to spend a lot of time discovering the many pleasures of this wonderful park.

The roads through *Golden Gate Park* are flat and wide, although there is a slight uphill grade heading into the park from the coast. Weekends usually find the park quite crowded with visitors enjoying the many points of interest within it. Sundays are especially good for cycling, since the roads are closed to car traffic.

Starting Point

Start the ride at the western end of the park at the corner of the Great Highway and John F. Kennedy Drive, near the Murphy Windmill. Get there by way of 19th Avenue by turning off at the 25th Avenue exit and proceeding through the park to the west end at the ocean.

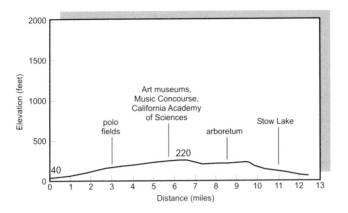

Mile Markers

0.0 Proceed EAST along John F. Kennedy Drive, heading into the park.

0.3 Continue STRAIGHT at the stop sign and then merge LEFT onto Martin Luther King Drive.

0.7 Continue STRAIGHT at the stop sign — South Lake will be on the left side.

0.9 Bear RIGHT to stay on Martin Luther King Drive.

2.1 Turn LEFT onto Middle Drive West just before 19th Avenue and then bear LEFT to stay on Middle Drive West.

3.0 Continue STRAIGHT at the stop sign — Polo Fields will be on the right side.

3.3 Turn RIGHT onto Martin Luther King Drive.

3.5 Turn RIGHT at the stop sign onto Chain of Lakes Drive.

3.7 Turn RIGHT onto John F. Kennedy Drive — Buffalo pen will appear on the left side.

5.0 Continue through the underpass beneath 19th Avenue.

5.7 Turn RIGHT onto Hagiwara Tea Garden Drive toward M.H. de Young Museum and the Japanese Tea Garden.

6.0 Turn LEFT onto Martin Luther King Drive and then turn LEFT again toward the California Academy of Science and the Steinhart Aquarium.

6.4 Turn RIGHT onto John F. Kennedy Drive.

6.8 Turn RIGHT onto Bowling Green Drive and then bear LEFT at the intersection.

7.2 Turn RIGHT onto Martin Luther King Drive.

7.5 Turn RIGHT to stay on Martin Luther King Drive.

8.2 Turn RIGHT toward Stow Lake.

8.8 Turn RIGHT just after the boathouse to continue around Stow Lake.

9.3 Turn RIGHT to get back on Martin Luther King Drive.

9.6 Continue STRAIGHT across 19th Avenue and then turn RIGHT onto Middle Drive West.

9.8 Bear RIGHT to get on Transverse Drive.

10.0 Turn LEFT onto John F. Kennedy Drive.

10.8 Turn RIGHT at the stop sign toward 30th Avenue and then turn LEFT onto a paved trail just before the park exit.

11.0 Spreckels Lake on the left side.

11.2 Turn LEFT at the stop sign and then RIGHT to get back on John F. Kennedy Drive.

11.6 Continue STRAIGHT at the stop sign.

12.0 Turn RIGHT at the stop sign at the end of John F. Kennedy Drive.

12.3 End of the ride back at the start point.

Conservatory of Flowers in Golden Gate Park

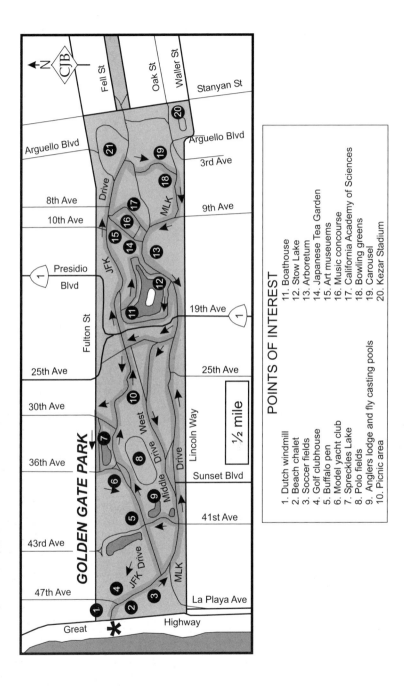

POINTS OF INTEREST

1. Dutch windmill
2. Beach chalet
3. Soccer fields
4. Golf clubhouse
5. Buffalo pen
6. Model yacht club
7. Spreckles Lake
8. Polo fields
9. Anglers lodge and fly casting pools
10. Picnic area
11. Boathouse
12. Stow Lake
13. Arboretum
14. Japanese Tea Garden
15. Art museuems
16. Music concourse
17. California Academy of Sciences
18. Bowling greens
19. Carousel
20. Kezar Stadium

4 San Francisco
Golden Gate Park and Lake Merced

Region: *Upper Peninsula*	**Distance:** *12 miles*
Ride Rating: *Easy*	**Elevation Gain:** *200 feet*
Type of Bike: *Road Bike*	**Riding Time:** *2 hours*

About the Ride

Golden Gate Park, the Great Highway, and Lake Merced highlight this ride in the western part of San Francisco. You may want to linger at the end to enjoy the sights and diversions which abound in *Golden Gate Park*. Lake Merced, located south of *Golden Gate Park* in Harding Park, is near the superb San Francisco Zoo and historic Fort Funston.

The route follows the Great Highway as it leads south along the coast to Harding Park. After completing loop around Lake Merced, it then leads back to *Golden Gate Park* along tree-lined Sunset Boulevard and then follows roads through the park a short distance to get back to the start point.

The route of this ride is generally quite flat. Substantial car traffic will be encountered and caution must be used at all times.

Starting Point

Start the ride at the western end of the park at the corner of the Great Highway and John F. Kennedy Drive, near the Murphy Windmill. Get there by way of 19th Avenue by turning off at the 25th Avenue exit and proceeding through the park to the west end at the ocean.

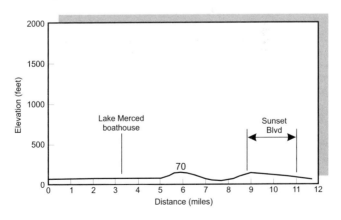

Facing page photo:
Dutch windmill in Golden Gate Park

Mile Markers

- 0.0 Proceed SOUTH along the Great Highway. Follow the bike path on the left side of the highway, just after you pass Golden Gate Park.
- 2.5 Cross Sloat Boulevard — bike path ends and you must cross the road and ride in the roadway.
- 3.3 Turn LEFT onto Skyline Boulevard. Lake Merced and Harding Park will be on the right side after the turn.
- 3.7 Turn RIGHT onto Lake Merced Boulevard.
- 4.2 Turn RIGHT where Sunset Boulevard intersects on the left to stay on Lake Merced Boulevard and continue around the lake.
- 6.2 Turn RIGHT onto John Muir Drive.
- 7.3 Bear RIGHT onto Skyline Boulevard.
- 7.8 Continue STRAIGHT at the intersection with the Great Highway on the left. This completes the loop around the lake.
- 8.5 Bear RIGHT to merge onto Sloat Boulevard.
- 8.7 Turn LEFT onto Sunset Boulevard.
- 10.9 Cross Lincoln Way to enter Golden Gate Park and then turn LEFT onto Martin Luther King Drive.
- 11.8 End of the ride back at the start point.

M.H. deYoung Museum in Golden Gate Park

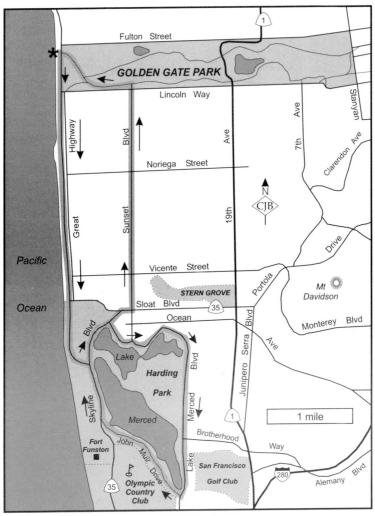

Ride No. 4

5 San Francisco
Angel Island Mountain Bike

Region: *Upper Peninsula*	**Distance:** *11 miles*
Difficulty Rating: *Easy*	**Elevation Gain:** *700 feet*
Skill Level: *Non- technical*	**Riding Time:** *2 hours*

About the Ride

One of the most unusual — and certainly one of the most pleasantly situated — state parks in California is *Angel Island State Park*. Located in San Francisco Bay, Angel Island has had a long and varied history. The earliest known use was as a home of native-Americans. Later, the island was used militarily in both the Civil War and World War II. It also served as an immigration center and for Nike missile defense. Today its use as a state park allows us to enjoy its unique beauty and to re-live its history through its museums and points of interest.

This ride starts at the dock area located at Ayala Cove, the place where the ferries arrive from San Francisco and Tiburon. It first circles about ¾ of the way around the island along a paved road. Spectacular views of the beautiful San Francisco Bay and fascinating points of interest along the way make this the kind of ride that needs to be done at a leisurely pace. The route then leads uphill along a wide fire road to a trail that also encircles the island. At the completion of this second loop, the route descends back to the paved road for the return to Ayala Cove.

The island has no public car traffic. The trails are smooth and the climbs are modest, allowing this ride to be done by beginners to the sport of mountain biking. The sights and history on the island should appeal to advanced riders as well, even though the ride itself is an easy one.

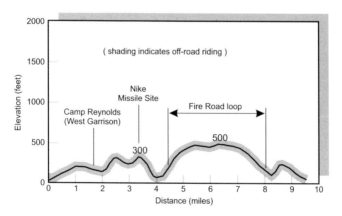

Starting Point

Access to Angel Island is by ferry, either from San Francisco or from Tiburon. From San Francisco, the *Blue and Gold Fleet* has regularly-scheduled trips leaving from Pier 41 (phone number is 415-773-1188) and from Tiburon, use the *Tiburon — Angel Island Ferry Company* (phone number is 415-435-2131). Call the ferry company you plan to use for schedules and directions.

Mile Markers

0.0 Proceed from the ferry dock to the right along the waterfront. Look for signs directing you to Perimeter Road.

0.2 Turn LEFT onto the bike path to head uphill toward Perimeter Road.

0.6 Turn RIGHT onto Perimeter Road.

1.4 Turn RIGHT into Camp Reynolds (West Garrison.) Proceed down to the water's edge at Point Stuart.

1.8 Turn around at Point Stuart.

2.2 Turn RIGHT back onto Perimeter Road.

2.6 Trail intersection on right side to Perles Beach.

2.7 Unmarked trail on the left side.

2.9 Old rock quarry on left side.

3.0 Turn LEFT toward Battery Drew.

3.3 Continue STRAIGHT ahead onto Perimeter Road.

3.7 Turn RIGHT at 4-way intersection to stay on Perimeter Road.

4.0 Nike missile site on the left side.

4.5 Continue STRAIGHT through Fort McDowell (East Garrison.).

4.7 Remains of old hospital on the left side.

5.0 Turn LEFT just after firehouse on the left side and proceed uphill on gravel road.

5.4 Bear RIGHT at the split to follow the posted bike route.

5.5 Continue along the fire road along the right side of the island water supply.

6.0 Trail intersection on the left side.

6.9 Another trail intersection on the left side.

7.3 Another trail intersection on the left side.

8.3 Turn LEFT on the paved road and then RIGHT to get back on the fire road.

8.7 Continue STRAIGHT at the end of the fire road loop and descend back to Perimeter Road.

9.1 Turn LEFT onto Perimeter Road.

10.3 Turn RIGHT sharply to get back on the bike path leading down into the cove.

10.7 End of the ride.

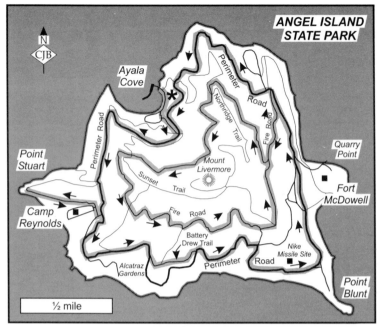

Ride No. 5

Ayala Cove on Angel Island

Woodside and the Mid-Peninsula

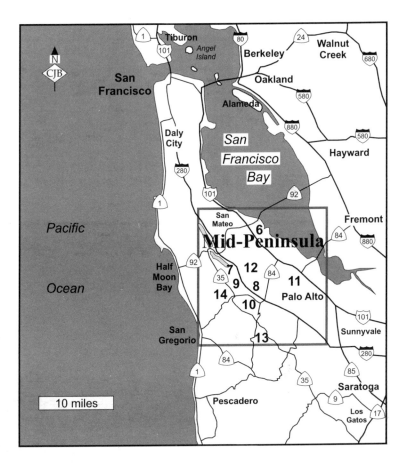

6   San Mateo
Foster City and San Mateo Bikeways

Region: *Mid-Peninsula*	**Distance:** *21 miles*
Ride Rating: *Easy*	**Elevation Gain:** *100 feet*
Type of Bike: *Road Bike*	**Riding Time:** *2 hours*

Ride Description

Foster City is a planned community built on in 1959 on landfill surrounding what was then Brewer Island. The Foster City Pedway/Bikeway follows a route leading around Foster City and connects with the San Mateo Pedway/Bikeway.

The route of this ride leads around Foster City initially along a lagoon and then along the Belmont Slough before reaching a levee on the shoreline of the bay. At the San Mateo Bridge (Highway 92) there is a fishing pier extending out over the water. Bikes are permitted in the pier. The route along the San Mateo Pedway/Bikeway passes Coyote Point, home of a picturesque yacht harbor and the Coyote Point Museum. Open to the public for a nominal fee, the museum offers an informative introduction to the ecology and environmental concerns of San Francisco Bay.

This ride is completely flat and nearly entirely along paved bike paths. Strong winds are often present and may make it seem like you are climbing.

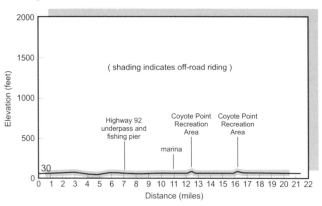

Starting Point

Start the ride in San Mateo, near the Fashion Island Shopping Center, at the intersection of Fashion Island Boulevard and Mariners Island Boulevard. To get there take Highway 101 to Foster City and get off at the exit for Hillsdale Boulevard. Follow Hillsdale Boulevard east to Edgewater Boulevard. Turn left on Edgewater Boulevard (which becomes Mariners Island Boulevard) to the intersection with Fashion Island Boulevard. Park anywhere nearby and start the ride at this intersection.

Mile Markers

0.0 Proceed WEST along Fashion Island Boulevard.

0.2 Turn LEFT to get on the Foster City Pedway/Bikeway, just before the bridge.

0.3 Highway 92 underpass.

1.2 Highway 92 underpass.

2.5 Continue STRAIGHT at the intersection with another bike path on the right.

4.9 Beach Park Boulevard on the left side of the bike path.

7.1 Highway 92 underpass and fishing pier.

8.5 Mariners Island Boulevard on the left side — continue STRAIGHT to get on the San Mateo Pedway/Bikeway.

9.0 Cross a bridge.

9.3 Bear RIGHT to stay on the bike path, heading toward the shoreline.

10.1 Bear RIGHT to cross a bridge and then turn RIGHT to stay on the bike path along the shoreline.

11.0 Turn RIGHT to continue on the bike path along the water edge.

11.2 Bear LEFT at the yacht harbor — Coyote Point Yacht Club building is on the left side. Then cross the road to continue along the bike path.

11.4 Turn RIGHT onto Coyote Point Drive.

11.7 At the end of the road, continue ahead onto the levee.

11.9 At the end of the bike path on the levee, turn around and return.

12.2 Turn RIGHT off the road to get back on the bike path at Eucalyptus Grove Picnic Area. Bikeway goes around the picnic area and then follows parallel to the road on the left.

12.7 Just after the animal shelter, turn RIGHT onto the road.

12.9 Turn LEFT to get back on the bike path.

13.5 Turn RIGHT onto Airport Boulevard.

14.1 Turn RIGHT onto Bayview Place toward the restaurant.

14.3 Get on the bike path at the far side of the restaurant and cross over a bridge. Then bear RIGHT to stay on the bike path along the shoreline.

14.5 At the hotel on the left side, turn around and return back the way you came.

20.2 Turn RIGHT off the bike path onto Mariners Island Boulevard.

21.1 End of the ride back at the start point.

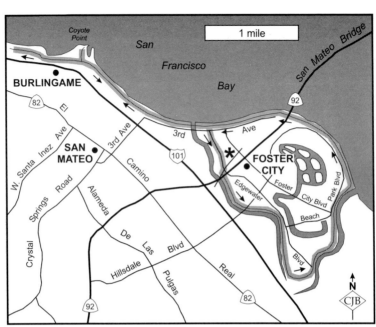

Ride No. 6

Coyote Point Yacht Harbor

7   San Mateo

Sawyer Camp Trail

Region: *Mid-Peninsula*	**Distance:** *12 miles*
Ride Rating: *Easy*	**Elevation Gain:** *250 feet*
Type of Bike: *Road Bike*	**Riding Time:** *1-2 hours*

About the Ride

Around the year 1400, considerably before Columbus set sail for America, a particular tree was beginning its life in what is now Northern California. Populated by Shoshone Indians, the region in which the tree was growing was in a pristine state, untouched by the progress and ravages of modern man. Some time later, in 1769, when the Spanish explorer, Don Gaspar de Potolá, became the first white man to set eyes on San Francisco Bay from Sweeney Ridge, that same California laurel tree (also known as a bay tree) was then over 400 years old and stood silent witness to the event, albeit at some distance from it. Today that tree, known as the Jepson Laurel, still stands and is passed by thousands of people each week as they relax and unwind from the tensions of modern life by traversing the Sawyer Camp Trail.

If trees could talk, this one could also tell the story of a man named Leander Sawyer, who in 1853, some 84 years after Portolá, bought the land around the area and established a trail leading to his home. Later, the trail was used by stagecoaches and ultimately became part of the main route between San Francisco and Half Moon Bay. After the flooding of Crystal Springs Reservoir in 1888 to serve the water needs of San Francisco, the road was used very little until 1978, when it was made into a recreation trail.

The Jepson Laurel, named in honor of Willis Linn Jepson, a noted botanist in California, is one of the highlights of this casual ride. Be sure to stop at the picnic site along the Sawyer Camp Trail to soak of the atmosphere around this notable tree.

The route is an out-and-back along the trail. It is generally quite flat except for a small hill near the end and the trail is paved the entire length. Because of the popularity of this trail with runners, walkers and cyclists, especially on weekends, it is imperative that caution by exercised at all times.

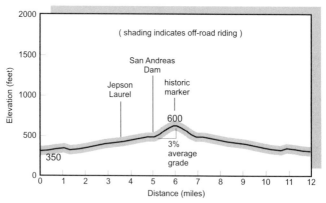

Starting Point

The Sawyer Camp Trail begins at the Lower Crystal Springs Reservoir in San Mateo, at the intersection of Crystal Springs Road and Skyline Boulevard. To get there, take Highway 280 to the Highway 92 interchange. Get off there and follow Highway 92 west toward Half Moon Bay for about ½ mile and then turn right onto Skyline Boulevard — Highway 35. Follow Highway 35 for about 1½ miles to the intersection with Crystal Springs Road.

Mile Markers

0.0 Proceed along the Sawyer Camp Trail by entering at the gate.

3.5 Picnic area on the left side — The Jepson Laurel, the oldest and largest laurel tree known in California, is located here.

4.8 Begin a short climb.

5.1 Cross over San Andreas Dam.

5.9 Information board on the left side.

6.0 Gate at the north end of the trail — return back the way you came.

12.0 End of the ride back at the start point.

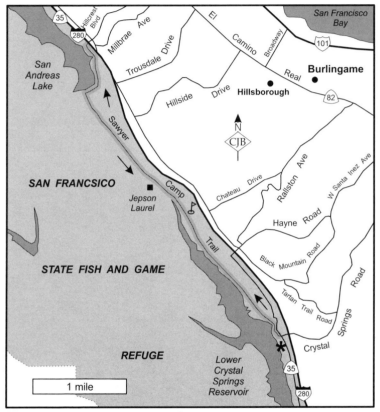

Ride No. 7

8   Woodside

Woodside to the Pulgas Water Temple

Region: *Mid-Peninsula*	**Distance:** *14 miles*
Ride Rating: *Easy*	**Elevation Gain:** *500 feet*
Type of Bike: *Road Bike*	**Riding Time:** *2 hours*

About the Ride

Far away from the Bay Area and within the boundaries of *Yosemite National Park* lies the Tuolomne River watershed. Each year, in the springtime, when the Sierra snows begin to melt and feed the many streams flowing into the Grand Canyon of the Tuolomne, the water accumulates behind the O'Shaughnessy Dam in the Hetch Hetchy Reservoir. Then, through a remarkable series of aqueducts, tunnels and powerhouses, the water is transported across the Central Valley and into Crystal Springs Reservoir, located just north of Woodside, to quench the thirst of the Bay Area. As a monument to this achievement, the Pulgas Water Temple serves to remind us of the precious nature of this resource.

The route of this ride leads out from the town of Woodside along Cañada Road to the water temple and then returns the same way. Just before getting back to Woodside, the route leads along some of the quiet residential roads around the town and past the historic Woodside Store and museum. Rolling hills with only a few easy climbs characterizes the terrain for the ride. Wide bike lanes are present along most of the route.

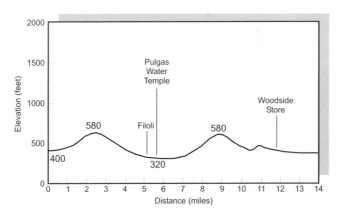

Facing page photo:
Jepson Laurel along Sawyer Camp Trail

Starting Point

Begin the ride at the historic Pioneer Hotel building in Woodside. To get there, take Highway 280 to Woodside and get off at the exit for Woodside Road (Highway 84). Follow [1]Woodside Road west a short distance to Woodside. Park behind or near the Pioneer Hotel at the intersection of Woodside Road and Whiskey Hill Road.

Mile Markers

0.0 Proceed WEST along Woodside Road toward central Woodside.

0.2 Turn RIGHT onto Cañada Road.

1.5 Freeway underpass.

3.2 Freeway underpass.

3.7 Edgewood Road intersection on the right side.

5.1 Entrance to Filoli Estate on the left side.

5.6 Pulgas Water Temple on the left — return back along Cañada Road when you are finished with your visit.

7.5 Edgewood Road intersection on the left side.

10.1 Turn RIGHT onto Olive Hill Lane.

10.5 Turn LEFT onto Albion Avenue.

11.0 Turn RIGHT onto Manuella Avenue.

11.4 Turn RIGHT onto Kings Mountain Road.

11.8 Turn LEFT onto Tripp Road — Woodside Store on the right side.

12.7 Turn LEFT onto Woodside Road.

14.0 Continue STRAIGHT through the intersection in central Woodside to stay on Woodside Road.

14.2 End of the ride back at the start point.

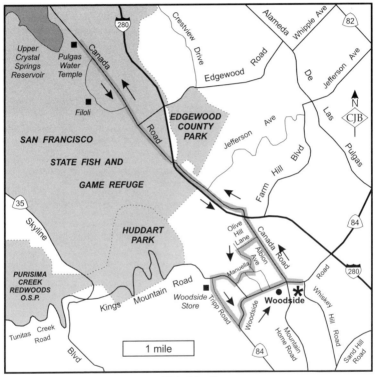

Ride No. 8

9   Woodside

Kings Mountain — Skyline Boulevard — Cañada Road Loop

Region: *Mid-Peninsula*	**Distance:** *23 miles*
Ride Rating: *Difficult*	**Elevation Gain:** *2000 feet*
Type of Bike: *Road Bike*	**Riding Time:** *3 hours*

About the Ride

The San Andreas Fault, one of the most famous faults in the world, extends from the vicinity of Point Arena in Northern California, all the way to Baja and passes directly through the Bay Area. San Andreas Lake and both Upper and Lower Crystal Springs Reservoirs lie directly on the fault line. The fault is actually a split between two major plates in the Earth's crust. Each plate experiences unsteady movement. The Pacific Plate, on the west, moves north, relative to the American Plate, on the east, about 1-2 inches per year.

Earthquakes occur when the plates fail to move for extended periods of time and the resulting stresses build to the point where a major slip suddenly results. This was the case in 1906 when the Great San Francisco Earthquake, centered near Point Reyes, occurred and the Pacific Plate lunged northward about 16 feet. The resulting shock waves traveled through the earth's core and recorded all over the world.

The route of this ride begins in Woodside and initially leads past the historic Woodside store before the major climb in the route takes place along Kings Mountain Road. At the top of Kings Mountain Road, the route then leads northward along Skyline Boulevard, with panoramic views in both directions. The long and gentle downhill ends at Highway 92 for the final drop down to the reservoirs and the return to Woodside along relatively flat Cañada Road.

Some car traffic should be expected along the demanding climb on Kings Mountain Road. Strong west-to-east crosswinds are common on the long descent on Skyline Boulevard and more traffic will be encountered on Highway 92.

Facing page photo:
Pulgas Water Temple

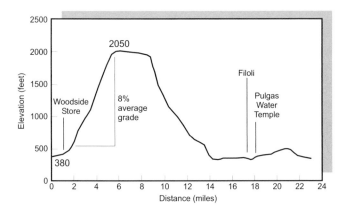

Starting Point

Start the ride in the town of Woodside. To get there, take Highway 280 to Woodside and get off at the exit for Woodside Road (Highway 84). Follow Woodside Road west a short distance to Woodside. Park near the town and start the ride at the intersection of Woodside Road and Cañada Road.

Mile Markers

0.0 Proceed WEST along Woodside Road.

0.8 Turn RIGHT onto Kings Mountain Road.

1.5 Historic Woodside Store and museum on the left side.

2.9 Huddart County Park entrance on the right side.

5.9 At the top of the climb, turn RIGHT onto Skyline Boulevard.

7.1 Mountain House Restaurant on the left side.

8.4 Parking area for Purisima Creek Redwoods Preserve on the left side.

12.9 Turn RIGHT onto busy Highway 92.

14.9 Continue STRAIGHT at the intersection with Skyline Boulevard (Highway 35) on the left.

15.6 Turn RIGHT onto Cañada Road.

18.0 Pulgas Water Temple on the right side.

18.4 Filoli Historic Center on the right side.

23.1 End of the ride back at Woodside.

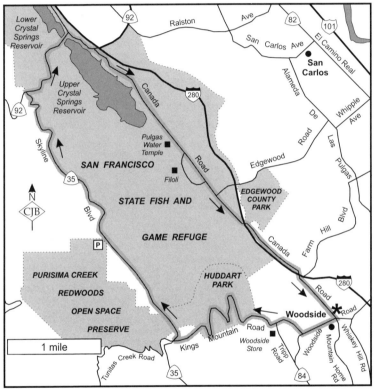

Ride No. 9

Woodside and the Mid-Peninsula

10 Woodside
Old La Honda Road

Region: *Mid-Peninsula*	**Distance:** *20 miles*
Ride Rating: *Difficult*	**Elevation Gain:** *2300 feet*
Type of Bike: *Road Bike*	**Riding Time:** *3-4 hours*

About the Ride

In 1869 a man came to live in Woodside to recuperate from an illness. His name was Robert Orville Tripp and he was a dentist. After his recovery from the illness, he decided to stay in Woodside and with a partner he established a lumber business. The timber was harvested in hills above and around Woodside and was shipped to San Francisco to assist in the rapid construction going on there at that time. In addition to the lumber business, he built a general store to serve the needs of the growing community. Functioning as a post office, general store, hotel, and stable, it also was a gathering place for locals. The original Woodside Store has been restored and today houses a museum with artifacts from old Woodside. It is located at the corner of Kings Mountain Road and Tripp Road.

The route of this ride begins in Woodside and is highlighted by a climb early in the ride up Old La Honda Road, a former logging road which today is used by several cycling clubs as a benchmark test to establish the climbing abilities of its members. The grade is a fairly constant 7% and has a well-defined beginning and end. Average climbers will take 30-40 minutes to complete the climb while the best can do it in as short a time as about 15 minutes.

After reaching the top of Old La Honda Road, the route follows Skyline Boulevard downhill to the intersection with Highway 84 and then climbs again before the final winding descent back to Woodside along Kings Mountain Road.

Starting Point

Begin the ride at the historic Pioneer Hotel building in Woodside. To get there, take Highway 280 to Woodside and get off at the exit for Woodside Road (Highway 84). Follow Woodside Road west a short distance to Woodside. Park behind or near the Pioneer Hotel at the intersection of Woodside Road and Whiskey Hill Road.

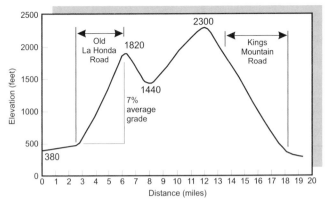

Mile Markers

0.0 Proceed WEST along Woodside Road toward central Woodside.

0.2 Turn LEFT onto Mountain Home Road.

2.2 Bear LEFT onto Portola Road and then turn RIGHT to stay on Portola Road — Sand Hill Road is to the left.

2.9 Turn RIGHT onto Old La Honda Road and begin climbing.

6.4 At the top of the hill, turn RIGHT onto Skyline Boulevard.

7.8 Continue STRAIGHT across Woodside Road — Highway 84.

12.2 Crest of the hill — 2,300 feet.

13.4 Turn RIGHT onto Kings Mountain Road and continue descent.

16.4 Huddart County Park on the left side.

17.8 Historic Woodside Store and museum on the right side.

18.5 Turn LEFT onto Woodside Road.

19.2 Continue STRAIGHT at intersection with Cañada Road on the left side and Mountain Home Road on the right.

19.4 End of the ride back at the start point.

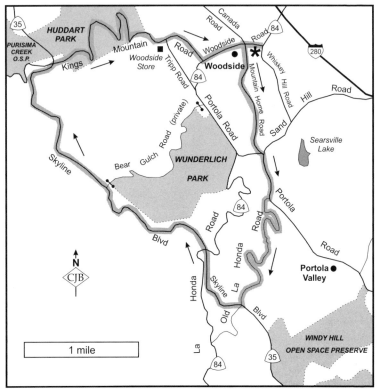

Ride No. 10

11   Palo Alto
Palo Alto and San Francisco by Train

Region: *Mid-Peninsula*	**Distance:** *49 miles*
Ride Rating: *Difficult*	**Elevation Gain:** *2000 feet*
Type of Bike: *Road Bike*	**Total Time:** *All Day*

About the Ride

A great way to experience nearly the entire Bay Area by bike is to utilize Caltrain to take you from Palo Alto into San Francisco and then to ride back. The train line ends in the city very near the Giants ballpark. The bike route from that point follows along the shoreline past the deep-water piers, Fisherman's Wharf, Fort Mason, the Marina Green, and into Crissy Field. From there, you will enter the Presidio and pass under the Golden Gate Bridge to get to the California Palace of the Legion of Honor. After that, the route leads to the historic Cliff House and then follows the Great Highway to Lake Merced. Skyline Boulevard then leads to the Sawyer Camp Trail for a leisurely cruise past the Upper and Lower Crystal Springs Reservoirs and then along Cañada Road to get to Woodside. Whiskey Hill Road and then Sand Hill Road take you to the Stanford University campus and then finally back to the Palo Alto train station.

Be sure to check with Caltrain for the train schedules, since they frequently change.

Although there are a number of small hills, the route of this ride is generally quite flat. There are no major climbs. The ride is fairly long in miles, but it goes fast because of the continuously changing scenery.

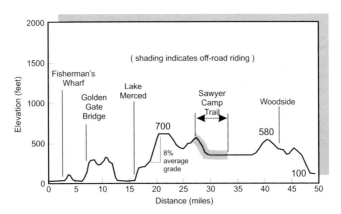

Starting Point

Begin the ride at the Caltrain station in Palo Alto on University Avenue, near Alma Street. To get there, take Highway 101 to Palo Alto and get off at the exit for University Avenue. Follow University Avenue west through downtown Palo Alto to the train station.

Mile Markers

0.0 Exit the Caltrain station on Fourth Street and proceed EAST on Fourth street and then take the first turn LEFT onto King Street.

1.1 Pass under the Bay Bridge.

1.6 Ferry Building on the right side.

3.2 Just after Pier 39, bear LEFT onto Jefferson Street.

3.5 Turn LEFT onto Hyde Street and climb the short hill and turn RIGHT onto Beach Street.

3.8 Turn LEFT onto Polk Street and then RIGHT onto North Point Street.

4.0 Turn LEFT onto Van Ness Avenue and then RIGHT onto Bay Street — Fort Mason is on the right side.

4.4 Turn RIGHT onto Laguna Street and continue around Fort Mason and then turn LEFT onto Marina Boulevard and follow the bike path which runs parallel to Marina Boulevard.

5.4 Just after the yacht harbor, continue STRAIGHT to enter Crissy Field.

5.8 Turn LEFT onto Halleck Street.

6.0 Turn RIGHT onto Lincoln Boulevard and then bear RIGHT to stay on Lincoln Boulevard — view of Golden Gate Bridge is directly ahead.

7.5 Just after the vista point parking on the right side, pass under the approach to the bridge.

9.2 Begin El Camino Del Mar.

10.1 Bear LEFT to go past the California Palace of the Legion of Honor.

10.5 At the bottom of the hill, turn RIGHT onto Clement Street.

10.9 Begin Seal Rock Drive.

11.3 Turn LEFT onto El Camino Del Mar and then RIGHT onto Point Lobos Avenue.

11.7 Cliff House on the right — begin descent to The Great Highway.

12.8 Continue along the bike path on the left side of the highway.

14.7 Cross Sloat Boulevard — bike path ends and you must cross the road and ride in the roadway.

15.6 Bear RIGHT to merge onto Skyline Boulevard — Highway 35.

19.7 Continue across the overpass for Highway 1.

24.8 Turn RIGHT off the road to get on a paved bike path running parallel to the road.

26.3 Bike path ends — turn left onto Larkspur Drive, cross under the freeway, and then turn RIGHT onto Skyline Boulevard.

26.9 Turn RIGHT onto Hillcrest Boulevard, cross under the freeway, and then get on Sawyer Camp Trail, a paved bike path.

32.9 At the end of the Sawyer Camp Trail, turn RIGHT onto Crystal Springs Boulevard.

34.5 Turn LEFT onto Highway 92 and then turn RIGHT onto Cañada Road.

36.9 Pulgas Water Temple on the right side.

38.5 Intersection with Edgewood Road on the left side.

42.0 Turn LEFT onto Woodside Road in central Woodside.

42.2 Turn RIGHT onto Whiskey Hill Road.

42.8 Turn LEFT onto Sand Hill Road.

44.1 Continue across the Highway 280 overpass.

45.7 Turn RIGHT onto Santa Cruz Avenue and then LEFT onto Junipero Serra Boulevard.

46.3 Turn LEFT onto Campus Drive West.

47.8 Turn LEFT onto Palm Drive.

48.5 End of the ride back at the Palo Alto Caltrain station.

California Palace of the Legion of Honor

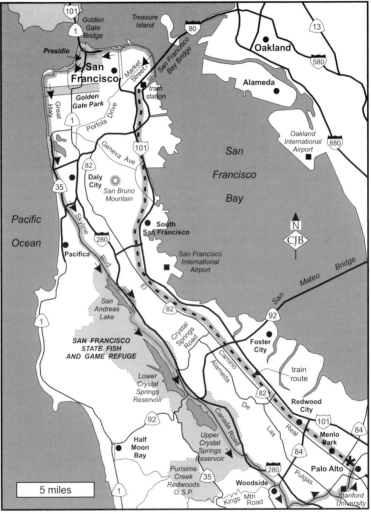

Ride No. 11

12 Woodside

Cañada Road and Alameda de Las Pulgas

Region: *Mid-Peninsula*	**Distance:** *16 miles*
Ride Rating: *Moderate*	**Elevation Gain:** *1000 feet*
Type of Bike: *Road Bike*	**Riding Time:** *2 hours*

About the Ride

The town of Woodside serves as the start and end of this ride. Formerly a center of extensive logging operations, Woodside today is a fashionable residential community and the home to many of the rich and famous of the Bay Area. While it is especially favored by those who prefer their recreation to be on the back of a horse, Woodside also has come to be the center of cycling activity as well. The weekends usually find the center of town to be a focal point for cyclists enjoying riding along the country roads and through the challenging hills surrounding the town.

This route follows initially along Cañada Road to Edgewood County Park. Edgewood Road then leads downhill through residential areas to Alameda de Las Pulgas ("Avenue of the Fleas"). After returning to Palo Alto, the route then climbs back up to Woodside along Sand Hill Road with a final stretch along quiet Manzanita Way.

The route is an easy one, even though there are some hills to climb. Bike lanes exist along most of the roads. Special care should be taken to obey all traffic laws, especially stop signs. Woodside law enforcement officers have historically been very strict, even for bicycles.

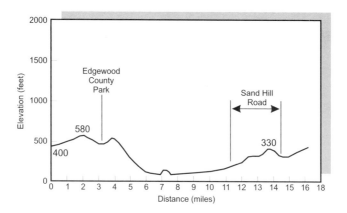

Starting Point

Start the ride in the town of Woodside. To get there, take Highway 280 to Woodside and get off at the exit for Woodside Road (Highway 84). Follow Woodside Road west a short distance to Woodside. Park near the town and start the ride at the intersection of Woodside Road and Cañada Road.

Mile Markers

0.0 Proceed NORTH along Cañada Road, heading away from Woodside.

1.3 Freeway underpass.

3.0 Freeway underpass.

3.5 Turn RIGHT onto Edgewood Road.

3.9 Freeway underpass.

4.8 Edgewood County Park on the right side.

5.2 Turn RIGHT onto Cordilleras Road.

5.9 Turn RIGHT onto Canyon Road.

6.6 Turn LEFT onto Highland Avenue and then LEFT onto Jefferson Avenue.

6.9 Turn RIGHT onto Alameda de Las Pulgas.

8.7 Cross Woodside Road.

9.7 Cross Atherton Avenue.

11.4 Turn RIGHT onto Sand Hill Road.

13.1 Freeway overpass.

14.4 Whiskey Hill Road intersection on the right side.

14.6 Turn RIGHT onto Manzanita Way.

15.9 Turn RIGHT onto Mountain Home Road.

16.3 End of the ride back at the start point.

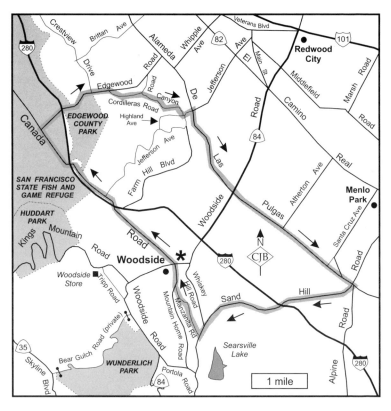

Ride No. 12

One of the many historic buildings in Woodside

13 Woodside

El Corte de Madera Mountain Bike

Region: *Mid-Peninsula*
Difficulty Rating: *Difficult*
Skill Level: *Very technical*

Distance: *10 miles*
Elevation Gain: *2200 feet*
Riding Time: *2-3 hours*

About the Ride

Car drivers cruising on a weekend morning along Skyline Boulevard above Woodside must wonder what is going on when they drive past Skegg's Point overlook. This is the time of peak activity for mountain bikers as the parking area is usually crowded with bikes and sometimes resembles a staging area for a bike race. Just across the road from Skegg's Point lies one of the most popular mountain bike destinations for advanced cyclists looking to improve their skills or simply to enjoy the challenges of the terrain in *El Corte de Madera Open Space Preserve*. The location of El Corte de Madera on the steep western slope of the Santa Cruz Mountains is what causes the trails to be so challenging. Bumpy, narrow and steep, the trails here are some of the most difficult around.

This ride follows a route through El Corte de Madera along some of its most popular trails. Single-track trails through thick forests and along constantly changing slopes provide both challenge and visual delights. Leading first along El Corte de Madera Creek Trail, the route descends and then crosses the creek. More gnarly sections along Resolution Trail and Fir Trail lead to a view point which serves as a good spot to rest and to catch your breath. Shortly after continuing, the route then leads to the Sandstone Formation, an unusual rock formation worth a side trip on foot. Manzanita, Timberview, and Crosscut Trails then lead to another place to stop. The old-growth Methuselah Tree is an example of what is not found much in the Santa Cruz Mountains — a redwood that somehow escaped the loggers. Looking to be in the neighborhood of 1,000 years old, the Methuselah Tree can be reached with a short walk down a well-marked path. Back on your bike, a fun-filled ride down Giant Salamander Trail is followed by a grunt of a climb back out of the preserve along Methuselah Trail.

The trails are mostly along narrow single-track. Steep terrain and often bumpy conditions make this one for skilled riders. Helmets are mandatory.

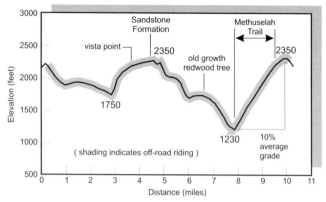

Starting Point

Start the ride at Skegg's Point overlook, located on Skyline Boulevard above Woodside. To get there from Woodside, head up Highway 84 out of Woodside and then turn right onto Kings Mountain Road. At the top, turn left on Skyline Boulevard and go about 2 miles to get to the overlook on the left side.

Mile Markers

0.0 Proceed NORTH out of the overlook parking area along the Skyline Boulevard and then turn LEFT into the preserve through gate number CM01. Continue STRAIGHT on the main trail.

0.2 Turn RIGHT onto El Corte de Madera Creek Trail.

0.9 Turn LEFT and cross over creek to stay on El Corte de Madera Creek Trail.

1.8 Bear RIGHT at the trail intersection with Tafoni Trail to stay on El Corte de Madera Creek Trail.

2.5 Turn LEFT onto Resolution Trail.

3.6 Turn LEFT onto Fir Trail.

3.7 Turn LEFT to the vista point for a view toward the west. Return from the vista point and get back on the Fir Trail to continue.

4.1 Turn LEFT onto the Tafoni Trail to see the Sandstone Formation which is about 0.1 miles up Tafoni Trail. Return from there and continue on the Fir Trail.

4.5 Turn RIGHT onto an unnamed trail to head toward Methuselah Trail.

4.6 Continue STRAIGHT at the intersection with Methuselah Trail to get onto Manzanita Trail.

5.8 Turn LEFT onto Timberview Trail.

6.0 Turn RIGHT onto Crosscut Trail.

6.1 Bear RIGHT to stay on Crosscut Trail.

6.5 Turn LEFT onto Timberview Trail.

6.7 Trail to the Methuselah Tree on the left side.

6.9 Turn RIGHT onto Giant Salamander Trail.

7.8 Turn RIGHT onto Methuselah Trail and begin steady climb out of the preserve.

9.5 Turn LEFT onto Fir Trail.

9.6 Turn RIGHT to stay on Fir Trail.

10.2 Turn RIGHT to get out of the preserve and onto Skyline Boulevard.

10.3 Back at the start point.

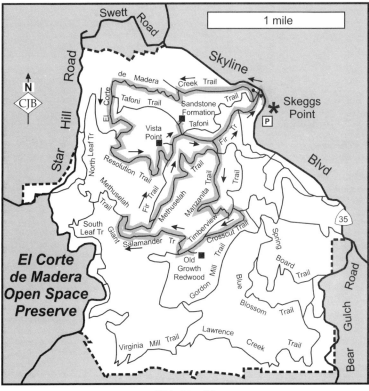

Ride No. 13

14   Woodside
Purisima Creek Redwoods Mountain Bike

Region: *Mid-Peninsula*	**Distance:** *7 miles*
Difficulty Rating: *Difficult*	**Elevation Gain:** *1600 feet*
Skill Level: *Very technical*	**Riding Time:** *2-3 hours*

About the Ride

The headwaters of the Purisima Creek form in the upper reaches of the Santa Cruz Mountains on the western slope. Following a path through lush redwood forests, the creek winds its way to the ocean at a point about 4 miles south of Half Moon Bay. The *Purisima Creek Open Space Preserve* consists of about 2,500 acres of public land open for the use of hikers, runners, equestrians and cyclists.

This ride follows a route around the preserve near its periphery and offers cyclists the full experience of the variety of terrain available there. The ride begins with a steady descent through the redwood forest along Whittemore Gulch Trail, a delightful single-track with moderate steepness. The return back up to Skyline Boulevard initially follows along a fairly flat route along the Purisima Creek Trail with numerous stream crossings over bridges. The trail then gets considerably steeper as it leads away from the creek. At the top of the climb, the route follows Skyline Boulevard the last two miles for the return back to the starting point.

Some rather steep sections of Purisima Creek Trail may require walking. Whittemore Gulch Trail is subject to seasonal closing during the wet winter months. In this case, the route can be changed by simply following Harkins Ridge Trail, an alternate way down the mountain.

Starting Point

Begin the ride at the main parking area for *Purisima Creek Redwoods*. To get there, take Highway 280 to Woodside and get off at the exit for Woodside Road (Highway 84). Follow Woodside Road west and through the center of Woodside and then turn right onto Kings Mountain Road. Follow Kings Mountain Road to the top of the mountains and turn right on Skyline Boulevard. The parking area is on the left side, about 2½ miles distant.

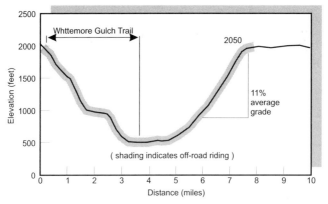

Mile Markers

  0.0 Proceed into the preserve at the main trailhead on the left side of the restrooms in the parking area at gate "PC01."

  0.3 Continue STRAIGHT ahead onto North Ridge Trail at the intersection with Harkins Ridge Trail on the left side.

  0.8 Turn LEFT onto Whittemore Gulch Trail and begin descent with numerous switchbacks.

  2.6 Cross a bridge.

  3.6 Bear RIGHT at the bottom of the hill to cross over bridge and then turn LEFT onto Purisima Creek Trail.

  4.6 Borden Hatch Mill Trail intersection on the right side.

  4.8 Cross a bridge.

  5.1 Cross another bridge.

  5.4 Cross another bridge.

  6.0 Soda Gulch Trail intersection on the left side.

  7.9 Pass through the gate and turn LEFT onto Skyline Boulevard.

10.0 End of the ride at the main parking area.

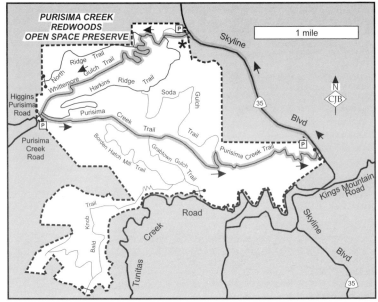

Looking toward the coast from Purisima Creek Redwoods Preserve

Palo Alto and the Lower Peninsula

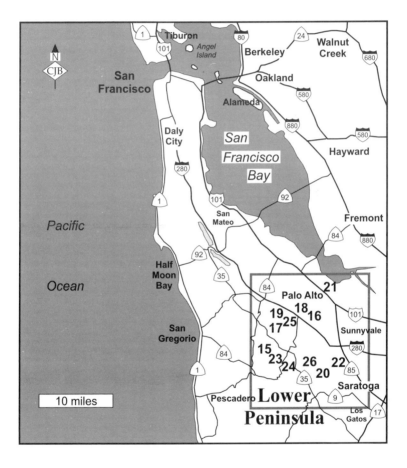

15   Palo Alto
Old La Honda Road and West Alpine Return

Region: *Lower Peninsula*	**Distance:** *35 miles*
Ride Rating: *Difficult*	**Elevation Gain:** *3700 feet*
Type of Bike: *Road Bike*	**Riding Time:** *3-5 hours*

About the Ride

One of the most popular cycling roads on the Peninsula — and in the entire Bay Area, for that matter — is Alpine Road in Palo Alto. Weekends find this road heavily traveled by bicycles with riders of all levels of ability. The local bike shops and cycling clubs know about Alpine Road and include it in recommended bike routes. Less well-known is the *other* Alpine Road, the one that exists on the other side of the mountains. Those in the know call it *West Alpine*. Blessed with very minimal car traffic and spectacular scenery, but cursed with a long and steep gradient, it doesn't get to see nearly as many bicycles. For those with the stamina and the desire, this is a ride that is not to be missed.

The route begins at the Park-and-Ride lot on Page Mill Road at the Highway 280 interchange. From there, it leads along Arastradero Road and Alpine Road toward Woodside. Just before Woodside, the route goes over the hills along Old La Honda Road and then leads to the tiny hamlet of La Honda. The return climb over the mountains is along West Alpine Road and then down Page Mill Road.

Two major climbs exist on this ride — one on Old La Honda Road (about 1,300 feet of vertical gain) and the other on West Alpine (about 2,100 feet up.) Both climbs are along roads with very little car traffic.

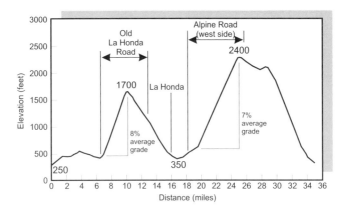

Starting Point

Begin the ride at the Park-and-Ride lot on Arastradero Road and Page Mill Road at the Highway 280 interchange for Page Mill Road. To get there, take Highway 280 to Palo Alto and get off at the exit for Page Mill Road. The parking area is on the west side of the freeway.

Mile Markers

0.0 Proceed WEST along Page Mill Road, heading away from the freeway.

0.3 Turn RIGHT onto Arastradero Road.

0.8 Arastradero Preserve parking on the right side.

2.3 Turn LEFT onto Alpine Road.

3.4 Turn RIGHT onto Portola Road.

6.4 Turn LEFT onto Old La Honda Road.

9.9 Continue STRAIGHT across Skyline Boulevard to stay on Old La Honda Road.

12.5 Turn LEFT onto La Honda Road (Highway 84).

16.0 La Honda — convenience store on the right side.

16.7 Turn LEFT onto Pescadero Road.

17.9 Bear LEFT onto Alpine Road — Pescadero Road continues to the right.

22.1 Bear LEFT to stay on Alpine Road — Portola State Park Road is on the right.

25.6 Continue STRAIGHT across Skyline Boulevard onto Page Mill Road.

26.2 Monte Bello Open Space Preserve parking area on the right side.

31.4 Moody Road intersection on the right side.

34.4 End of the ride back at the start point.

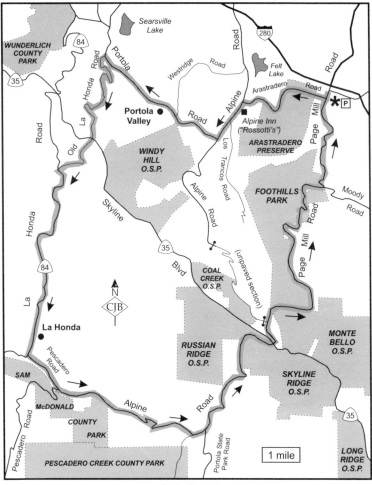

Ride No. 15

16   Los Altos
Los Altos — Stanford — Los Altos Bike Path

Region: *Lower Peninsula*	**Distance:** *17 miles*
Ride Rating: *Easy*	**Elevation Gain:** *900 feet*
Type of Bike: *Road Bike*	**Riding Time:** *2 hours*

About the Ride

The Stanford University campus, affectionately referred to as "The Farm," was originally the property of Leland and Jane Stanford and was, in fact, the Palo Alto Stock Farm and was operated by the Stanfords as a horse breeding ranch in the late 1800's. One of early California's most prominent citizens, Leland Stanford gained his early fame and fortune as the head of the Central Pacific Railroad. Later, he became governor and then a United States senator. The Stanford's' only son, Leland, Jr., died of typhoid in 1884 at the age of 15. As a memorial to their beloved son, the family founded the university, using their farm as the site for the campus. The property covers over 8,000 acres, stretching from the flatlands of the Santa Clara Valley up into the foothills of the Santa Cruz Mountains.

At the heart of the campus is the Inner Quadrangle, often referred to as the "Main Quad." The twelve original university classroom buildings and the Memorial Church surround the quad. The architecture on campus, a blend of Romanesque and Mission Revival styles, was carefully selected to blend in harmoniously with climate and landscape of northern California.

The route of this ride leads from Los Altos through residential areas of Los Altos Hills to the Stanford campus. A circuitous route through the university offers a chance to see the campus highlights and leads to a bike path for the return to Los Altos. Although there is a substantial hill along Arastradero Road, the remainder of the ride is mostly flat and suggests a leisurely pace.

Starting Point

Begin the ride in downtown Los Altos at the intersection of Main Street and Third Street. To get there, take Highway 280 to Los Altos and get off at the exit for El Monte Road. Proceed east on El Monte to Foothill Expressway. Turn left on Foothill Expressway and then right on San Antonio Road. Turn left on Whitney Street and then right on Third Street. Parking is plentiful in this area.

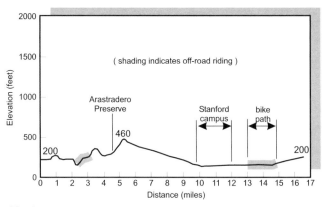

Mile Markers

0.0 Proceed WEST on Main Street and cross Foothill Expressway.

0.3 Turn RIGHT onto Old Altos Road and then RIGHT again onto Fremont Road.

1.4 Turn RIGHT to stay on Fremont Road.

2.3 Turn LEFT at Arastradero Road and get on the bike path on the right side.

3.2 At the end of the bike path, turn RIGHT onto Arastradero Road and cross under the freeway.

3.8 Turn LEFT onto Page Mill Road.

4.1 Turn RIGHT to resume Arastradero Road.

4.6 Arastradero Preserve parking on the right side.

6.0 Turn RIGHT onto Alpine Road.

7.9 Freeway underpass.

9.1 Turn RIGHT onto Junipero Serra Boulevard.

9.7 Turn LEFT onto Campus Drive West.

10.0 Turn RIGHT onto Santa Teresa Street.

10.4 Turn LEFT onto Samuel Morris Way and then turn RIGHT to follow a pathway — Panama Mall — through the campus.

10.6 The pathway ends. Proceed past the posts and turn LEFT onto Duena Street. Turn RIGHT immediately onto Escondido Mall and then LEFT along a small pathway leading to the Main Quad, where Memorial Church is located.

10.7 Continue through the Main Quad — the big plaza where the church entrance is located — and out toward the road. Turn RIGHT on the road — Serra Mall — and continue past Hoover Tower, on the right side.

11.0 Continue around a roundabout and pass the posts onto the main road — Serra Street.

11.5 Turn RIGHT on Campus Drive East.

11.7 Turn LEFT onto Escondido Road.

12.0 Continue past the posts.

12.1 Turn RIGHT onto Stanford Avenue and LEFT onto Hanover Street.

12.6 Cross Page Mill Road.

13.0 Turn LEFT to get on the bike path, just after the point where Hanover Street makes a sharp right turn.

13.2 Cross a road and continue on the bike path.

13.6 Turn LEFT at the junction in the bike path — Veterans Hospital is off to the right at this point.

13.7 Continue STRAIGHT to stay on the bike path leading around the left side of Gunn High School.

14.3 Turn LEFT onto Arastradero Road and then turn RIGHT to resume the bike path, just after the cemetery.

14.9 End of the bike path — turn RIGHT onto Los Altos Avenue.

15.3 Turn LEFT onto Edith Avenue.

16.5 Turn RIGHT onto Third Street.

16.7 End of the ride back at the start point.

Modern Sculpture in Los Altos

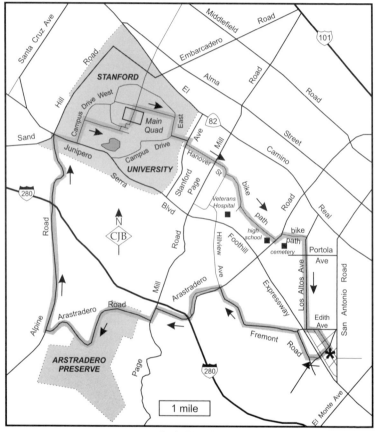

Ride No. 16

17 Portola Valley
Portola Valley Loop

Region: *Lower Peninsula*
Ride Rating: *Easy*
Type of Bike: *Road Bike*

Distance: *19 miles*
Elevation Gain: *900 feet*
Riding Time: *2 hours*

About the Ride

Mention that you are riding "The Loop" to a cyclist in Palo Alto and you are likely to get an immediate response of understanding. Easily the most popular bike ride in the area, the route is heavily followed on weekends and no directions are really necessary. You only have to find someone who rides at a comfortable pace and follow along.

The route of this ride generally follows the more traditional route of "The Loop," but some changes and some additional roads have been included to spice it up a bit. Beginning at a shopping center along Alpine Road in Ladera, the route initially follows Alpine Road towards the hills. Passing by the old and historic Alpine Inn — formerly "Rossotti's," or just "Zott's" — it leads past Portola Road and then back to Portola Road through a peaceful residential area. Portola Road ultimately takes you to Woodside, but first passes by the historic Woodside Store and its museum filled with artifacts from old Woodside. The return to Ladera follows along peaceful Manzanita Way and then Sand Hill Road to get back to Alpine Road.

There are some small hills along the way, but the ride is generally quite easy.

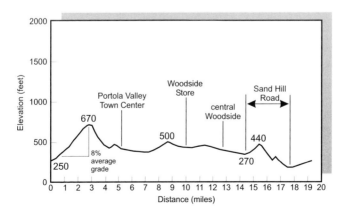

Starting Point

Begin the ride at the Ladera Shopping Center in Portola Valley. To get there, take Highway 280 to Portola Valley and get off at the exit for Alpine Road. Go west on Alpine Road for about ½ mile and park in the shopping center on the right side.

Mile Markers

0.0 Proceed WEST on Alpine Road.

1.4 Arastradero Road intersection on the left side.

2.7 Continue STRAIGHT through the intersection with Portola Road. Be sure to make a complete stop at the intersection, since traffic rules are strictly enforced in Woodside.

3.7 Turn RIGHT onto Willowbrook Drive.

4.5 Turn LEFT onto Portola Road.

5.1 Portola Valley Town Center on the left side.

7.2 Turn LEFT to stay on Portola Road — Sand Hill Road is to the right.

8.0 Bear RIGHT onto Woodside Road.

9.1 Turn LEFT onto Tripp Road.

10.0 Turn RIGHT onto Kings Mountain Road.

10.4 Turn LEFT onto Manuella Avenue.

10.8 Turn LEFT onto Albion Avenue.

11.3 Turn RIGHT onto Olive Hill Lane.

11.7 Turn RIGHT onto Cañada Road.

12.6 Continue through the intersection in Woodside to get on Mountain Home Road.

13.0 Turn LEFT onto Manzanita Way.

14.3 Turn LEFT onto Sand Hill Road.

17.5 Turn RIGHT onto Junipero Serra Boulevard and then bear RIGHT onto Alpine Road.

19.3 End of the ride back at the start point.

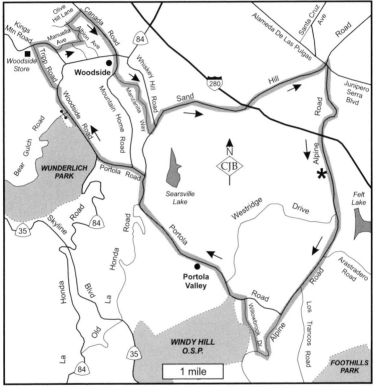

Ride No. 17

18   Los Altos
Los Altos — Stanford — Moody Road

Region: *Lower Peninsula*	Distance: *21 miles*
Ride Rating: *Moderate*	Elevation Gain: *1100 feet*
Type of Bike: *Road Bike*	Riding Time: *2 hours*

About the Ride

This ride takes some of the most pleasant routes around Los Altos and the Stanford University campus and then adds a little climb toward the end of the ride along Page Mill Road to challenge intermediate cyclists with an enhanced workout.

The route initially leads away from Lincoln Park, near downtown Los Altos, along quiet residential roads and then follows a pleasant bike path to get to the campus of Stanford University. After an easy cruise through the campus, it then leads up the gentle grade along Alpine Road to Arastradero Road. A rolling ride along Arastradero Road takes you to Page Mill Road, where you climb to get to Moody Road. Moody Road is quite steep and this route follows the preferred direction, namely down. After passing the campus of Foothill College, the route follows El Monte Road and then University Avenue to get back to Lincoln Park.

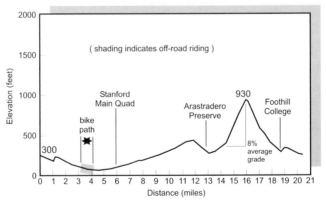

Starting Point

Begin the ride in Los Altos at Lincoln Park, just off Foothill Expressway. To get there, take Highway 280 to Los Altos and get off at the exit for El Monte Road. Follow El Monte Road east to Foothill Expressway and then turn left on Foothill Expressway. Turn left on Main Street and then left immediately on University Avenue. Lincoln Park will be on the left side. Park nearby and begin the ride at the intersection of University Avenue and Main Street (Burke Road).

Mile Markers

0.0 Proceed NORTH along University Avenue, heading parallel to Foothill Expressway.

0.3 Turn LEFT onto West Edith Avenue.

0.5 Turn RIGHT onto Fremont Road.

1.0 Turn RIGHT onto Manuella Road.

2.3 Turn RIGHT onto Arastradero Road and continue across Foothill Boulevard.

2.5 Turn LEFT onto the road leading in to Henry M. Gunn High School and continue along the bike path beginning at the end of the road.

3.2 Turn RIGHT at the "T" intersection to stay on the bike path.

3.6 Continue across Matadero Avenue to stay on the bike path.

3.8 Turn RIGHT onto Hanover Street at the end of the bike path.

4.1 Continue STRAIGHT across Page Mill Road.

4.4 Cross California Avenue and go past the auto barriers to stay on Hanover Street.

4.6 Turn RIGHT onto Stanford Avenue and then LEFT onto Escondido Road.

4.7 Continue past the auto barriers at the intersection with Comstock Circle.

5.1 Continue STRAIGHT across Campus Drive East.

5.4 Turn RIGHT at Galvez Street and then LEFT onto Serra Street. Follow Serra Street past the roundabout and through the Stanford campus.

5.8 The Main Quad is on the left and Palm Drive on the right.

6.1 Turn LEFT onto Via Ortega and then RIGHT onto Panama Street.

6.6 Turn LEFT onto Campus Drive.

7.3 Turn RIGHT onto Junipero Serra Boulevard.

7.9 Turn LEFT onto Alpine Road.

9.1 Cross under the freeway.

11.0 Turn LEFT onto Arastradero Road.

12.5 Parking area for Arastradero Preserve on the left side — restrooms.

13.1 Turn RIGHT onto Page Mill Road.

15.0 Altamont Road intersection on the left side.

15.4 Entrance to Foothills Park on the right side.

15.6 Turn LEFT onto Moody Road.

18.2 Altamont Road intersection on the left side.

18.4 Continue STRAIGHT onto the campus roads for Foothill College. Turn RIGHT onto the main campus loop and then RIGHT again to get back out to Moody Road

18.8 Turn LEFT onto Moody Road.

19.0 Cross through Highway 280 underpass.

19.7 Turn LEFT onto University Avenue — before you get to Foothill Boulevard.

20.4 End of the ride back at the start point.

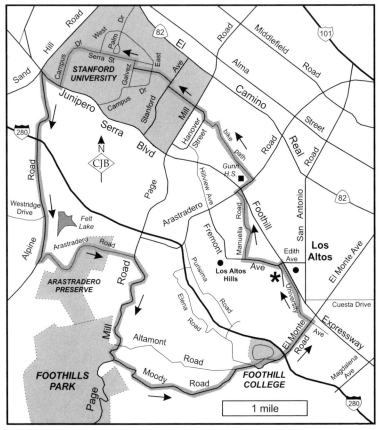

Ride No. 18

Facing page photo:
Hoover Tower on Stanford campus

19 Los Altos
Tour of Los Altos Hills

Region: *Lower Peninsula*	**Distance:** *14 miles*
Ride Rating: *Easy*	**Elevation Gain:** *600 feet*
Type of Bike: *Road Bike*	**Riding Time:** *2 hours*

About the Ride

The quaint town of Los Altos, by virtue of its numerous restaurants and shops and its access to plenty of free parking, is a very pleasant place to start and end a bike ride.

The route begins by following busy Foothill Expressway south toward Cupertino. After about 2½ miles, the route heads into the residential neighborhoods of Los Altos Hills. After passing the prestigious Los Altos Hills Country Club, the route continues past numerous luxurious homes on its way to Foothill College. After a loop around the campus, the route then begins its only substantial climb — up along Altamont Road. From the top, you will be rewarded with panoramic views of the valley below. The return to downtown Los Altos passes by picturesque orchards and then by stables and a little league ball field.

Foothill Expressway can be quite busy with car traffic, but a wide bike lane makes it quite comfortable. While there is a substantial climb along Altamont Road, the rest of the route is mostly flat and light with traffic.

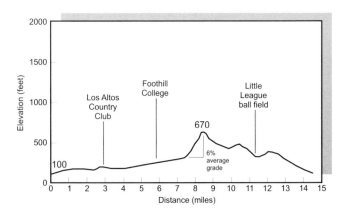

Starting Point

Begin the ride in downtown Los Altos at the intersection of Main Street and Third Street. To get there, take Highway 280 to Los Altos and get off at the exit for El Monte Road. Proceed east on El Monte to Foothill Expressway. Turn left on Foothill Expressway and then right on San Antonio Road. Turn left on Whitney Street and then right on Third Street. Parking is plentiful in this area.

Mile Markers

0.0 Proceed WEST on Main Street toward Foothill Expressway and turn LEFT onto Foothill Expressway.

2.6 Turn RIGHT at Loyola Drive exit and turn RIGHT immediately and then bear LEFT to go up the hill on Loyola Drive.

2.9 Country club on the right side.

3.3 Begin Fairway Drive.

3.8 Turn LEFT onto Hillview Drive.

4.0 Continue STRAIGHT across Magdalena Avenue.

4.4 Turn RIGHT onto Hilltop Drive and then LEFT onto Summerhill Avenue.

5.2 Turn LEFT onto El Monte Road.

5.8 After crossing under the freeway, turn RIGHT into the Foothill College campus.

6.0 Turn RIGHT at the stop sign — Perimeter Road — to go around the campus.

6.9 Turn RIGHT at the stop sign to exit the campus and get on Moody Road, and then bear LEFT immediately to stay on Moody Road

7.2 Turn RIGHT onto Altamont Road.

8.3 Turn RIGHT onto Taaffe Road and begin descent.

9.2 Turn LEFT onto Elena Road.

11.0 Turn RIGHT onto Purissima Road.

11.9 Turn LEFT onto Concepcion Road.

12.8 Turn RIGHT onto Fremont Road.

13.7 Turn LEFT onto Edith Avenue.

13.9 Cross Foothill Expressway.

14.2 Turn RIGHT onto Third Street.

14.4 End of the ride back at Main Street.

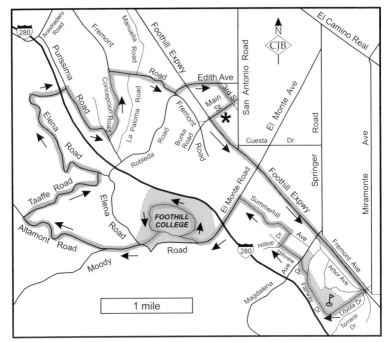

Ride No. 19

View from Altamonte Road in Los Altos Hills

20 Cupertino
Stevens Canyon Out-and-Back

Region: *Lower Peninsula*	**Distance:** *20 miles*
Ride Rating: *Moderate*	**Elevation Gain:** *1100 feet*
Type of Bike: *Road Bike*	**Riding Time:** *2-3 hours*

About the Ride

The *Stevens Creek* and *Upper Stevens Creek County Parks*, and *Monte Bello Open Space Preserve* all offer outdoor recreation for a wide variety of interests. Hikers, mountain bikers, and equestrians share the trails in those parks and preserves nestled below and in Stevens Canyon. Fishermen enjoy the delights provided by the Stevens Creek Reservoir, fed by Stevens Creek which comes down through the canyon.

This ride is an easy-to-follow one which leads generally along Stevens Creek to the end of Stevens Canyon Road. The end of the road is the beginning of the trails into *Monte Bello*. The route leads initially along Foothill Expressway from the residential areas of Cupertino. As the road climbs gradually you will pass by the parking area for *Stevens Creek County Park* and then Stevens Creek Dam and Reservoir. After that, the scenery gets more natural as you enter the canyon and continue to climb along a gentle grade. From the end of the road, the return back follows the way you went in and is generally downhill.

A challenging option popular with cyclists who follow this route regularly is to climb up Montebello Road, located at the 3.4 mile mark in the ride directions. This road climbs about 2,000 feet in about 5 miles. The steepest parts are in the beginning and at the end. The views at the top make the climb one to remember.

Starting Point

Begin the ride in a shopping center at Homestead Road and Foothill Expressway in Cupertino. Take Highway 280 to Cupertino and get off at the exit for Foothill Expressway just north of the Highway 85 interchange. Follow Foothill Expressway north a short distance and then turn right on Homestead Road. Park in the shopping center and begin the ride on Foothill Expressway.

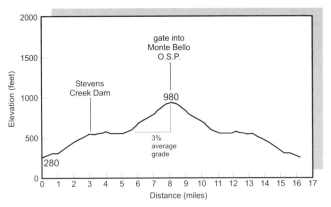

Mile Markers

0.0 Proceed WEST along Foothill Expressway, heading toward the freeway.

0.2 Freeway underpass.

1.1 Continue across Stevens Creek Boulevard.

1.6 Intersection with McClellan Road on the left side — begin Stevens Canyon Road.

2.3 *Stevens Creek County Park* on the left side.

3.0 Stevens Creek Dam on the left side.

3.4 Intersection with Montebello Road on the right side.

4.6 Bear RIGHT at the intersection with Mount Eden Road on the left to stay on Stevens Canyon Road.

6.3 Intersection with Redwood Gulch Road on the left side.

8.2 End of the road at the gate for *Monte Bello Open Space Preserve* — return the way you came.

16.4 End of the ride back at the start point.

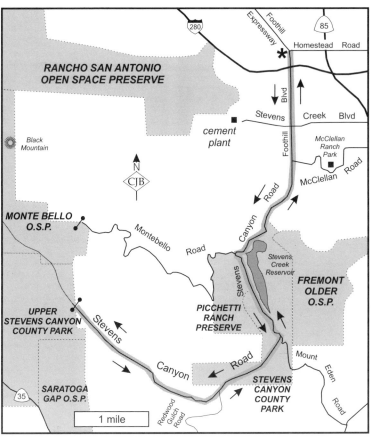

Ride No. 20

21 Mountain View
Shoreline Park and Palo Alto Baylands

Region: *Lower Peninsula*	**Distance:** *19 miles*
Ride Rating: *Easy*	**Elevation Gain:** *Flat*
Type of Bike: *Road Bike*	**Riding Time:** *2 hours*

About the Ride

Starting at the train station near downtown Mountain View, this route initially leads along Stevens Creek on the Stevens Creek Trail, a paved bike path that follows the creek toward the bay. At the bay, the bike path connects to a paved path which leads through *Mountain View Shoreline Park*. Built on reclaimed land using modern landfill techniques, *Shoreline Park* includes a municipal golf course, a sailing lake, and Shoreline Amphitheatre, an outdoor stage for world-class entertainers. Trails through the park offer rare glimpses of nesting and migrating shorebirds as well as stunning views of San Francisco Bay and the hills and mountains across the water in the East Bay. Walkers, runners, and cyclists share the trails, so it is important to be considerate and courteous at all times.

Just north of Shoreline Park is the *Palo Alto Baylands Preserve.* A network of paved trails leads through the wetlands and around *Palo Alto Municipal Airport* and a golf course. The return to Mountain View follows surface roads with well-marked bike lanes for safety. The ride is completely flat and is best enjoyed at a leisurely pace with frequent stops to observe the wildlife and the scenery.

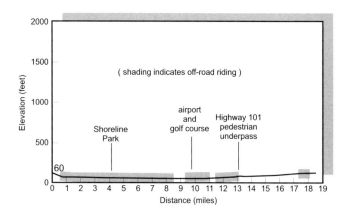

Starting Point

Begin the ride at the Mountain View train station. To get there, take Highway 85 south from Highway 101 and get off at the exit for Central Expressway. Turn right onto Central Expressway and then left onto Castro Street. Turn left onto Villa Street and then left again onto Hope Street. The train station is on Evelyn Avenue.

Mile Markers

0.0 Proceed EAST along Evelyn Avenue, heading away from downtown Mountain View.

0.5 Just before Highway 85, turn RIGHT to get on the Stevens Creek Trail. Bear RIGHT to get on the overpass to cross Central Expressway, heading toward the bay.

1.0 Highway underpass.

1.5 Cross over a road and continue on the bike path.

1.9 Highway underpass.

3.3 End of the Stevens Creek Trail. Turn LEFT to continue on the bike path leading into *Shoreline Park.*

4.3 Turn RIGHT to continue on the bike path along the side of the road in Shoreline Park. The golf course is on the far side of the road.

4.7 Cross a bridge and turn RIGHT onto the bike path and then turn RIGHT again almost immediately to head toward the bay shore-line.

5.4 Bear RIGHT at the trail split.

5.8 Turn RIGHT to continue on a dirt trail along the levee — Adobe Creek Loop Trail goes to the left.

7.7 Cross over flood control dam.

7.9 Continue STRAIGHT at the trail junction — Adobe Creek Loop Trail goes to the left.

8.3 Turn RIGHT onto the road — this is Harbor Road.

8.5 Continue STRAIGHT at the intersection with Embarcadero Road on the left side — airport is on the left side.

8.7 Duck pond on the left side.

9.0 Cross over a bridge and turn LEFT on the gravel bike path to enter the *Palo Alto Baylands Preserve.* The Interpretive Center will be on the right side.

9.3 Trail turns RIGHT to lead around the airport.

9.9 Turn LEFT at the end of the runway.

10.8 At the end of the bike path, continue through the parking lot and then turn LEFT onto Embarcadero Road and then RIGHT onto Faber Place. Continue on the bike path which begins at the end of Faber Place and follow it as it leads parallel to the frontage road.

12.9 Turn LEFT to follow the Benjamin Lefkowitz Bicycle/Pedestrian Underpass to go under Highway 101. On the far side, continue on Fabian Way and then turn RIGHT onto East Meadow Drive and then LEFT to continue along East Meadow Drive.

14.7 Cross San Antonio Road and bear RIGHT to stay on Middlefield Road — Old Middlefield Road goes to the left.

15.4 Cross Rengstorff Avenue.

16.3 Cross Shoreline Boulevard.

17.1 Cross over Highway 85 and then turn RIGHT onto Stevens Creek Bike Path.

17.6 Turn RIGHT to get on the overpass over Central Expressway and then turn LEFT onto Evelyn Avenue.

18.4 End of the ride back at the train station.

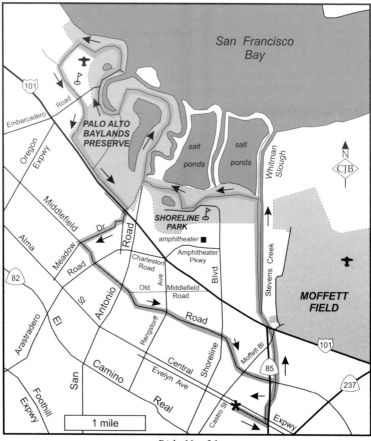

Ride No. 21

22   Cupertino
Cupertino — Saratoga — Redwood Gulch

Region: *Lower Peninsula*	**Distance:** *16 miles*
Ride Rating: *Moderate*	**Elevation Gain:** *1300 feet*
Type of Bike: *Road Bike*	**Riding Time:** *2-3 hours*

About the Ride

In the 1930's the Santa Clara Valley was much different than it is today. Orchards and ranches dominated the valley, earning it the nickname, "The Valley of Heart's Delight." Prominent among these was the McClellan Ranch in Cupertino. Today, much of the original ranch is preserved along McClellan Road. The ranch house and the barn give the visitor a sense of what life was like back then. Two additional historic buildings — The Baer's Blacksmith Shop and the water tower from the Parish Ranch — were moved from other sites nearby to preserve them here, adding to the appeal of *McClellan Ranch Park*.

The De Anza College campus serves as the starting point for this ride. The route takes you first through residential areas of Cupertino and Saratoga and past the Mountain Winery, site of a summer concert series. After that comes the main climb of the ride along Congress Springs Road (Highway 9) to get to Redwood Gulch Road and the steep descent into Stevens Canyon. Stevens Canyon Road then leads through the beautiful canyon along Stevens Creek to Stevens Canyon Dam and Reservoir. The final stretch back to De Anza College is along McClellan Road and passes the historic McClellan Ranch.

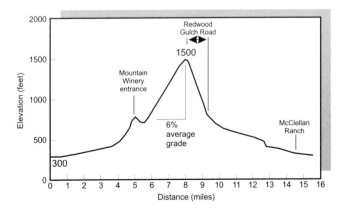

Starting Point

Start the ride at De Anza College in Cupertino, at the intersection of McClellan Road and Stelling Road. From Highway 85, take the Stevens Creek Boulevard exit and head east on Stevens Creek Boulevard past the De Anza College campus. Turn right on Stelling Road and proceed to the intersection with McClellan Road. Park where convenient and start the ride at the intersection.

Ride Details and Mile Markers

0.0 Proceed SOUTH along Stelling Road, heading away from De Anza College.

0.5 Cross over Highway 280.

1.6 Continue STRAIGHT as Stelling Road becomes Prospect Road.

1.9 Turn RIGHT onto Via Roncole.

2.2 Via Roncole becomes Arroyo de Arguello.

2.6 Continue STRAIGHT across Wardell Road.

3.0 Turn LEFT onto Comer Drive and then RIGHT onto Pierce Road.

4.5 Intersection with Mount Eden Road on the right side.

5.2 Entrance for Mountain Winery on the right side. This is the venue for a summer concert series.

5.5 Turn RIGHT onto Congress Springs Road (Highway 9).

6.2 Intersection for Sanborn Skyline County Park on the left side.

7.5 Booker Creek Road intersection on the left side.

8.0 Turn RIGHT onto Redwood Gulch Road and prepare for steep descent.

9.4 Turn RIGHT onto Stevens Canyon Road.

11.0 Bear LEFT at the intersection with Mount Eden Road on the right side.

12.4 Montebello Road intersection on the left side.

14.2 Turn RIGHT onto McClellan Road.

14.6 Historic McClellan Ranch Park on the left side.

15.6 Highway 85 overpass.

15.8 End of the ride at Stelling Road.

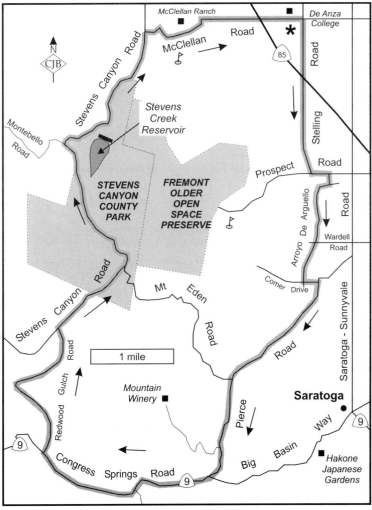

Ride No. 22

23   Palo Alto
Russian Ridge Mountain Bike

Region: *Lower Peninsula*	**Distance:** *11 miles*
Difficulty Rating: *Moderate*	**Elevation Gain:** *1300 feet*
Skill Level: *Somewhat technical*	**Riding Time:** *2-3 hours*

About the Ride

At the top of the Santa Cruz Mountains, at the intersection of Skyline Boulevard and Page Mill Road, lie four separate open space preserves. *Russian Ridge*, *Coal Creek*, *Monte Bello* and *Skyline Ridge* preserves are all administered by the Midpeninsula Regional Open Space District. When considered in total, the area of the four preserves forms one of the largest places in the Bay Area where cyclists, hikers and equestrians can sample the pleasures of the outdoors. A special benefit is that the preserves are already located at the mountain top, so extensive climbing is not needed to get there. The panoramic views come without the heavy price of a long climb.

This ride tours both Russian Ridge and Coal Creek and covers about 11 miles of trails through mountain meadows and coastal forests. Substantial climbing is required, as the trails follow along rolling mountain ridges for most of the route. Whereas wide fire trails predominate in Russian Ridge, Coal Creek presents some challenges associated with narrow single-track. About 1 mile along Skyline Boulevard is necessary to make the connection between the two preserves.

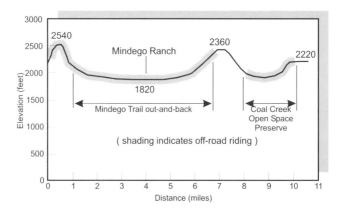

Starting Point

Start the ride at the parking lot for *Russian Ridge Open Space Preserve*. To get there, take Highway 280 to Palo Alto and get off at the exit for Page Mill Road. Follow Page Mill Road west all the way to the top at Skyline Boulevard. Cross Skyline Boulevard and go into the parking lot on the right side.

Mile Markers

0.0 Proceed NORTH out of the parking lot on Ridge Trail, heading toward Borel Hill.

0.6 Bear RIGHT to stay on Ridge Trail.

0.8 Bear LEFT to stay on Ridge Trail — Borel Hill is to the right.

1.5 Turn LEFT and LEFT again to get on Mindego Ridge Trail.

1.8 Alder Spring Trail intersection on the right side.

3.3 Turn RIGHT on the fire road to stay on Mindego Ridge Trail.

4.4 Turn AROUND at the end of the trail at Mindego Ranch and return along Mindego Ridge Trail.

5.5 Turn LEFT to continue returning along Mindego Ridge Trail.

7.1 Continue STRAIGHT at the intersection with Ridge Trail to get to Skyline Boulevard and the turn LEFT onto Skyline Boulevard.

7.8 Turn RIGHT onto unmarked and easy-to-miss Crazy Pete's Road. This road can be found by looking for the sign as you turn onto the road indicating Coal Creel Preserve.

8.1 Begin gravel road and pass through gate marked "CC06." Then enter Coal Creek at the gate marked "CC04." Turn RIGHT immediately after the gate to stay on Crazy Pete's Road toward Alpine Road.

8.4 Bear RIGHT at the intersection with Valley View Trail on the left to stay on Crazy Pete's Road.

9.2 Turn RIGHT to stay on Crazy Pete's Road.

9.5 Turn RIGHT after the barrier onto Alpine Road.

10.7 Turn RIGHT after the barrier onto Page Mill Road.

11.2 Cross Skyline Boulevard.

11.3 End of the ride at the parking area.

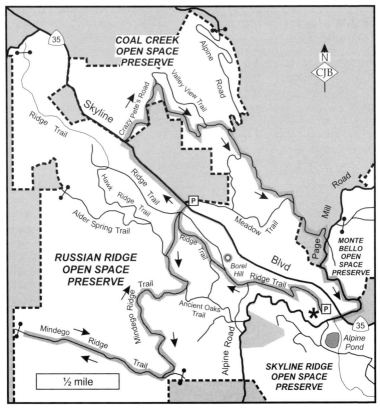

Ride No. 23

24   Palo Alto

Skyline Ridge Mountain Bike

Region: *Lower Peninsula*
Difficulty Rating: *Moderate*
Skill Level: *Somewhat technical*

Distance: *7 miles*
Elevation Gain: *1200 feet*
Riding Time: *2 hours*

About the Ride

Skyline Ridge Open Space Preserve and the upper portion of *Monte Bello Open Space Preserve* are the areas covered by this ride. Located high in the Santa Cruz Mountains above Palo Alto, these preserves are just a portion of the land administered by the Midpeninsula Regional Open Space District.

The route actually begins in the parking lot for yet another preserve, Russian Ridge, located just across Alpine Road from Skyline Ridge. It leads across Alpine Road and immediately past a small pond and then up a hill into Skyline Ridge. Panoramic views into Monte Bello at the top of the hill are followed by a descent toward Horseshoe Lake. After passing the lake the route continues through the parking area for Skyline Ridge and then across Skyline Boulevard into Monte Bello. The trail through Monte Bello takes you down into the canyon which forms the watershed for Stevens Creek. Canyon Trail leads back up the hill and then some single-track leads through meadows back to Skyline Boulevard and the return to the start point.

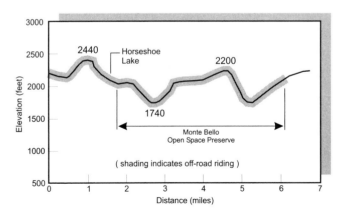

Starting Point

Start the ride at the parking lot for *Russian Ridge Open Space Preserve*. To get there, take Highway 280 to Palo Alto and get off at the exit for Page Mill Road. Follow Page Mill Road west all the way to the top at Skyline Boulevard. Cross Skyline Boulevard and go into the parking lot on the right side.

Mile Markers

0.0 Cross Alpine Road to get to the trailhead into Skyline Ridge.

0.1 Continue past the barrier to get on Alternate Ridge Trail toward Horseshoe Lake.

0.2 At Alpine Pond, bear RIGHT to stay on the bicycle-only trail around the lake and then turn LEFT on the paved road.

0.4 Dirt trail begins just after private residences.

0.6 Turn LEFT to stay on Alternate Ridge Trail.

1.0 Continue STRAIGHT at the major trail intersection.

1.4 Horseshoe Lake on the right side.

1.5 Continue past the gate and through the equestrian parking lot and turn LEFT onto the trail leading to the main parking area.

1.7 Just past the main parking area, turn LEFT and cross Skyline Boulevard to reach the trailhead into Monte Bello. Just past the gate marked "MB06," bear LEFT and follow the trail as it runs parallel to the road

2.1 Continue STRAIGHT at the trail intersection on the left.

2.3 Continue STRAIGHT toward Canyon Trail at another trail intersection on the left side.

2.9 Turn LEFT onto Canyon Trail and begin climb toward Page Mill Road.

3.6 Trail intersection on the left.

3.8 Turn LEFT just before the gate and follow this trail parallel to the road.

4.0 Continue through the parking lot for Monte Bello along the trail running parallel to the road.

4.5 Bear LEFT at the trail split toward Skyline Boulevard.

5.5 Turn RIGHT at the end of the trail and continue toward Skyline Boulevard.

5.9 Exit Monte Bello and turn RIGHT onto Skyline Boulevard.

6.6 End of the ride at the parking area for Russian Ridge.

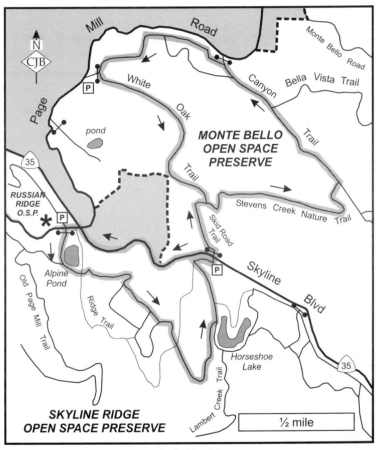

Ride No. 24

25   **Palo Alto**
Arastradero Preserve Mountain Bike

Region: *Lower Peninsula*	**Distance:** *5 miles*
Difficulty Rating: *Easy*	**Elevation Gain:** *600 feet*
Skill Level: *Somewhat technical*	**Riding Time:** *1-2 hours*

About the Ride

With its relatively small hills and with trails that alternate between single-track and fire road, and with its close proximity to Palo Alto, *Arastradero Preserve* is an ideal place for the beginner mountain bike enthusiast to practice skills and to develop endurance. Plentiful trees along Arastradero Creek and around the lake provide for welcome shade on hot summer days.

Administered by the city of Palo Alto, *Arastradero Preserve* is a popular destination for hikers, runner and equestrians, as well as cyclists. Courteous behavior is essential to making multi-use preserves work.

This easy tour of the preserve is offered as a simple introduction to mountain biking. Small hills and some narrow trails allow the beginner cyclist to develop basic riding skills without the need to tackle extended climbs. This route leads from the main parking area for the preserve along a variety of trails past the lake, along the creek, and up and down some small hills for a complete tour around the preserve.

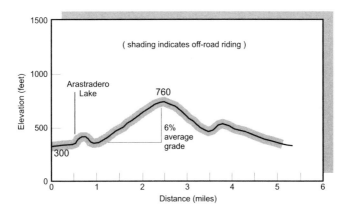

Starting Point

To get to *Arastradero Preserve*, take highway 280 to Palo Alto and get off at the exit for Page Mill Road. Head west on Page Mill Road for about ¼ mile and then turn right onto Arastradero Road. The parking area is about ½ mile down along Arastradero Road.

Mile Markers

0.0 From the parking area, proceed along Gateway Trail, the trail that goes parallel to Arastradero Road in the general direction toward Page Mill Road.

0.1 Cross the road to get into the main area of the preserve and continue along Juan Bautista de Anza Trail.

0.4 Bear LEFT at the intersection with Meadowlark Trail on the right side to stay on Juan Bautista de Anza Trail.

0.6 Arastradero Lake is on the left side. Turn LEFT and follow Paseo del Roble Trail to Lake Trail for a view of the lake. Return back and then continue along Juan Bautista de Anza Trail.

0.9 Turn LEFT just past the lake onto Arastradero Creek Trail.

1.4 Turn RIGHT onto Acorn Trail and climb a short hill.

1.8 Turn LEFT to continue on Meadowlark Trail.

2.3 Continue STRAIGHT at the intersection with Woodrat Trail on the left side and then look for the trail on the right which goes a short distance to a vista point.

2.6 Turn LEFT onto Bowl Loop.

2.9 Turn LEFT onto Bowl Loop Trail.

3.3 Turn LEFT to get back onto Meadowlark Trail.

3.4 Turn RIGHT onto Woodland Star Trail.

3.8 Turn RIGHT and then LEFT to get on Bay Laurel Trail.

3.9 Bear LEFT onto Ohlone Trail.

4.1 Turn RIGHT onto Juan Bautista de Anza Trail.

4.3 Turn LEFT to get back onto Meadowlark Trail.

4.7 Turn LEFT onto Portola Pastures Trail.

4.9 Turn RIGHT to head toward the road.

5.1 Turn RIGHT onto Arastradero Road.

5.3 End of the ride back at the parking area.

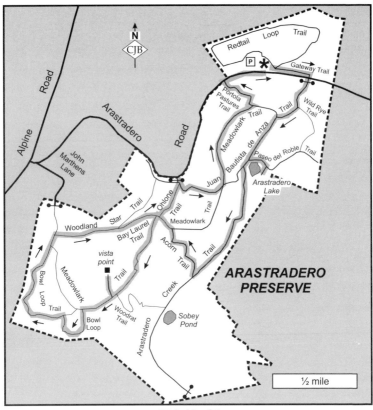

Ride No. 25

In the Arastradero Preserve

26   Cupertino
Monte Bello Preserve Mountain Bike

Region: *Lower Peninsula*	**Distance:** *17 miles*
Difficulty Rating: *Difficult*	**Elevation Gain:** *2500 feet*
Skill Level: *Somewhat technical*	**Riding Time:** *3-4 hours*

About the Ride

The upper Stevens Creek watershed, from the grassy slopes of Monte Bello Ridge to the brush and oak-covered woodlands below, is contained within the *Monte Bello Open Space Preserve*. Located in the Santa Cruz Mountains high above Cupertino, Monte Bello is the largest preserve managed by the Midpeninsula Regional Open Space District. While the primary access into the preserve is on Page Mill Road about one mile from Skyline Boulevard near the top of the mountain range, there are other ways to get in as well.

This ride utilizes one of those entry points. Starting well below Monte Bello at Stevens Creek Reservoir, the route leads uphill immediately along paved Montebello Road. After a long climb, the road ends and a trail leads into the preserve, climbing some more until it reaches the top of Black Mountain, the site of microwave communication towers.

After passing the communication towers, the route then descends into Stevens Canyon along Indian Creek Trail, affording stunning views of the hills and valleys which form the watershed. The descent continues along Stevens Canyon Trail and finally exits the preserve onto Stevens Canyon Road for the easy return to the start point.

Starting Point

The ride starts in Cupertino on Stevens Canyon Road just past Stevens Creek Dam. Follow Highway 280 and take the exit for Foothill Expressway and Grant Road. Note that there are several exits for Foothill Expressway, so be sure to take the one in Cupertino, not far from the Highway 85 interchange. Continue west along Foothill Boulevard and cross Stevens Creek Boulevard. Keep going as the road name changes to Stevens Canyon Road. Continue past the dam to a small parking area on the left side of the road just after the intersection with Montebello Road. Park here to begin the ride.

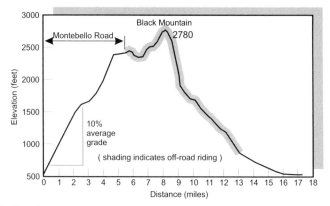

Mile Markers

0.0 Proceed EAST on Stevens Canyon Road, back toward the dam and turn LEFT onto Montebello Road. Begin climbing immediately.

5.2 Turn LEFT and pass through gate "MB08" onto Water Wheel Trail.

6.6 Turn LEFT to onto Monte Bello Road (fire road.)

7.8 Black Mountain summit at the microwave towers — elevation is 2,780 feet.

8.0 Turn LEFT onto Indian Creek Trail.

8.2 Continue STRAIGHT at the trail intersection on the right side.

8.8 After a long descent, turn LEFT onto Stevens Canyon Trail.

10.8 Continue STRAIGHT at the intersection with Grizzly Flat Trail on the right side.

11.2 Turn Continue STRAIGHT at the intersection with Table Mountain Trail on the right side.

12.5 Continue past the gate onto Stevens Canyon Road.

14.4 Continue STRAIGHT at the intersection with Redwood Gulch Road on the right side.

16.1 Continue STRAIGHT at the intersection with Mount Eden Road on the right side.

17.3 End of the ride at the parking area.

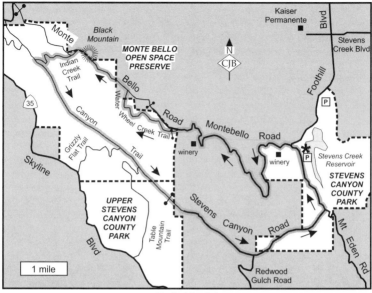

Ride No. 26

Water Wheel Creek Trail in Monte Bello Preserve

Along the Coast and on the Western Slope

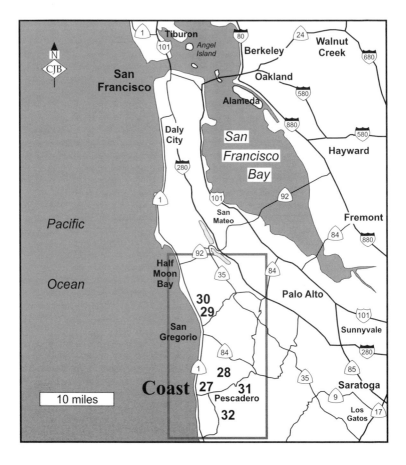

27   Pescadero

Pescadero and Pigeon Point Lighthouse

Region: *Pacific Coast*
Ride Rating: *Moderate*
Type of Bike: *Road Bike*

Distance: *28 miles*
Elevation Gain: *1400 feet*
Riding Time: *3-4 hours*

About the Ride

Pescadero is a small agricultural town about two miles inland from the Pacific Coast and about directly west of Woodside. Its quaint country charm is enhanced by small country churches, antiques shops, and several notable restaurants. Just outside of town is the *Pescadero Marsh Natural Preserve*, a key link in the chain of coastal wetlands stretching along the Pacific coast of North America. These wetlands are home to many species of birds, mammals, and fishes, and serve as essential resting places for the many migratory birds traveling north and south along the Pacific Flyway. Hiking trails through the marsh lead to observation points for viewing the wildlife there.

South of Pescadero along Highway 1, the Pigeon Point Lighthouse is one of the most photographed along the coast. Beaming its beacon to offshore vessels for more than 100 years, the lighthouse today also is the site of a youth hostel, an inexpensive refuge for travelers. Occasionally there are guides at the lighthouse to give tours and descriptions.

The route of this ride initially leads out of Pescadero along Stage Road. A series of small hills quickly gets you warmed up as you head toward San Gregorio. At San Gregorio, the route heads to Highway 1 on the coast and then south along the highway toward *Pescadero Marsh* and then on to Pigeon Point Lighthouse. Just after the lighthouse, the route leads inland once again and passes by *Butano State Park* along Cloverdale Road as it takes you back to Pescadero.

Starting Point

Start the ride in Pescadero, about 16 miles south of Half Moon Bay. To get there, take Highway 280 to Woodside and get off at the exit for Highway 84 (Woodside Road). Follow Highway 84 west through Woodside and over the hill to La Honda. In La Honda, turn left onto Pescadero Road and follow it to Pescadero. Begin the ride at the intersection of Pescadero Road and Stage Road in the heart of Pescadero.

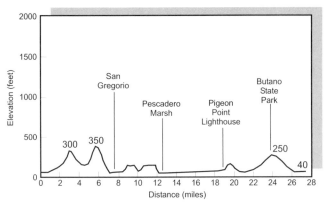

Mile Markers

0.0 Proceed NORTH along Stage Road.

4.8 Intersection with Pomponio Road on the right side.

7.5 Turn LEFT in San Gregorio onto La Honda Road (Highway 84).

8.3 Turn LEFT onto Highway 1, heading south.

11.1 *Pomponio State Beach* on the right side.

13.0 Continue STRAIGHT at the intersection with Pescadero Road, on the left side.

15.9 Intersection with Bean Hollow Road on the left side.

18.7 Pigeon Point Lighthouse on the right side.

21.0 Turn LEFT onto Gazos Creek Road.

23.1 Turn LEFT onto Cloverdale Road as Gazos Creek Road continues straight ahead.

23.4 *Butano State Park* entrance on the right side.

25.4 Intersection with Canyon Road on the right side.

26.7 Turn LEFT onto Pescadero Road.

27.3 End of the ride in Pescadero.

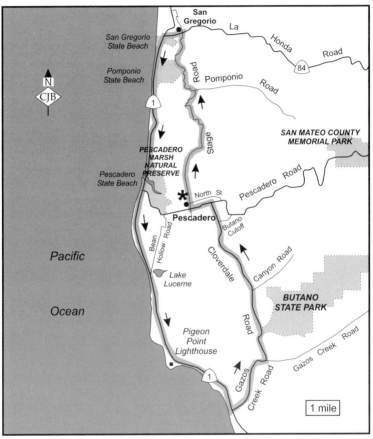

Ride No. 27

28   Pescadero

La Honda — San Gregorio — Pescadero Loop

Region: *Pacific Coast*	**Distance:** *28 miles*
Ride Rating: *Moderate*	**Elevation Gain:** *1600 feet*
Type of Bike: *Road Bike*	**Riding Time:** *3 hours*

About the Ride

This classic loop on the western slope of the Santa Cruz Mountains takes you through three small towns: La Honda, San Gregorio, and Pescadero, each with its own flavor and personality. Standing in sharp contrast to the two other towns along the route, La Honda has the feel of a remote mountain town, by virtue of the dense forests and the rural nature of the structures there. The route initially leads west along a gentle downward grade on La Honda Road to San Gregorio. The Peterson and Alsford General Store, a fixture in San Gregorio for over 100 years, offers refreshment and a wide variety of merchandise. It is common to see bicyclists and motorcyclists mingling at the store on busy weekends. The route then heads toward Pescadero along Stage Road. Two small hills get your heart beating a bit as you follow Stage Road to Pescadero.

Pescadero is the largest of the three towns on the route, but still retains the small-town charms that have characterized the community for over 100 years. Antique shops and quaint churches give the town a resemblance to those in New England. Once out of town, however, the resemblance ends as the hillsides and farmlands remind you again of the uniqueness that is northern California. The route out of Pescadero follows Pescadero Road and has a gentle upgrade at first as it passes through the tiny hamlet of Loma Mar and then past *San Mateo County Memorial Park*. The major climb of the ride leads to the high point along the route of about 1,000 feet, at Haskins Ridge. From the crest of the hill, you can view the Butano forest in the distance toward the south. The final descent through the redwood forest finally brings you back to La Honda.

Facing page photo:
Eucalyptus along Stage Road

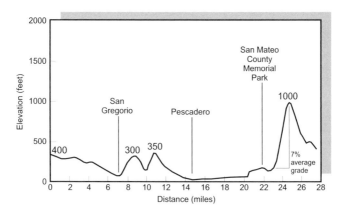

Starting Point

Start the ride in La Honda, where there are several stores and restaurants with adequate parking. To get there, take Woodside Road (Highway 84) from Woodside up and over the hill, where it becomes La Honda Road, to La Honda. Begin the mileage at the corner of La Honda Road and Pescadero Road.

Mile Markers

0.0 Proceed WEST on La Honda Road (Highway 84) toward the coast.

5.4 Intersection with Bear Gulch Road on the right side.

7.3 Turn LEFT in San Gregorio onto Stage Road.

9.1 First summit — 300 feet.

10.9 Second summit — 350 feet side.

14.6 Turn LEFT in Pescadero onto Pescadero Road.

15.2 Intersection with Cloverdale Road on the right side.

16.0 Intersection with Butano Cut-Off on the right side.

20.7 Loma Mar store on the right side.

22.0 Entrance to *San Mateo County Memorial Park* on the right side.

24.5 Crest of the hill — 1,000 feet.

26.2 Turn LEFT to stay on Pescadero Road — Alpine Road is to the right.

27.4 End of the ride in La Honda.

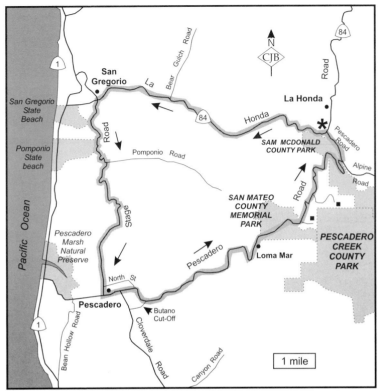

Ride No. 28

Ranch near Pescadero on Stage Road

29 Half Moon Bay
Tunitas Creek Road

Region: *Pacific Coast*	**Distance:** *29 miles*
Ride Rating: *Difficult*	**Elevation Gain:** *2200 feet*
Type of Bike: *Road Bike*	**Riding Time:** *3-4 hours*

About the Ride

A delightful seaside resort community, Half Moon Bay has for many years been a favorite destination for people in both San Francisco and the Santa Clara Valley. Its popular annual events include a Portuguese Festival in the spring and the famous Pumpkin Festival in the fall. The Clam Chowder and Chili Cook-Off and annual Harbor Day, both in the summer, are events also worth attending.

The route leads south from Half Moon Bay along Highway 1 and then goes inland as it follows along quiet and rolling Verde Road. A 4-mile section along Lobitas Creek Road leads past country homes and ranches as it climbs toward Tunitas Creek Road. The deep redwood forests which line Tunitas Creek Road contrast sharply with the rolling hills prevalent around Half Moon Bay. The lack of major car traffic and the tranquil surroundings make the climb a memorable one.

At the top, the route follows Skyline Boulevard north along the ridge of the mountains. Spectacular views in both directions highlight this gradual descent toward Highway 92. Crosswinds are common along Skyline Boulevard, as the air masses move from the coast to the inland parts of the Bay Area.

The final return back to Half Moon Bay is along busy Highway 92. Riding downhill will get you there quickly and you may even be able to keep up with the cars along some sections.

This ride is a challenging one by virtue of the extended climb along Tunitas Creek Road. The crosswinds that sometimes occur along Skyline Boulevard and the car traffic on Highway 92 can be nuisances, but they cannot take away from the overall beauty of this ride.

Starting Point

Start the ride in downtown Half Moon Bay at the intersection of Highway 92 and Main Street. To get there, take Highway 280 and get off at the exit for Highway 92 toward Half Moon Bay. Take Highway 92 west and continue until just before the end at the intersection with Highway 1. There is ample parking in this area.

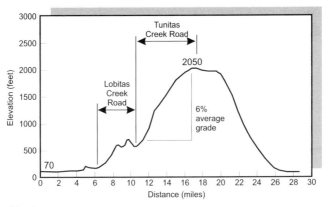

Mile Markers

0.0 Proceed SOUTH along Main Street, going directly through town.

1.3 Turn LEFT to head south on Highway 1.

4.5 Turn LEFT onto Verde Road — this is the first of three places where Verde Road comes out to Highway 1.

4.9 Turn RIGHT to stay on Verde Road — Purisima Creek Road continues straight ahead.

6.3 Continue STRAIGHT at the Verde Road access spur to Highway 1 on the right.

6.5 Turn LEFT onto Lobitas Creek Road.

10.7 Turn LEFT onto Tunitas Creek Road.

15.3 Star Hill Road intersection on the right side.

16.6 Turn LEFT onto Skyline Boulevard at the top of the hill.

17.7 Kings Mountain Fire Station on the right side.

19.2 Purisima Creek Redwoods Preserve on the left side.

23.6 Turn LEFT onto busy Highway 92 (Half Moon Bay Road).

25.4 Cross Pilarcitos Creek.

28.6 End of the ride in Half Moon Bay.

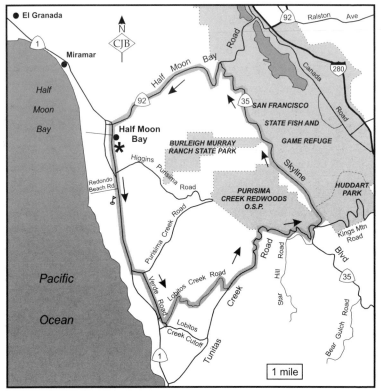

Ride No. 29

30   San Gregorio

San Gregorio and Half Moon Bay

Region: *Pacific Coast*	**Distance:** *28 miles*
Ride Rating: *Moderate*	**Elevation Gain:** *2800 feet*
Type of Bike: *Road Bike*	**Riding Time:** *2 hours*

About the Ride

The Peterson and Alsford General Store, a fixture in San Gregorio for over 100 years, has long been a meeting place for locals as well as travelers and visitors. It is common to see bicyclists, motorcyclists, and touring motorists mingling at the store on busy weekends. In the cold winter months, there is usually a warm fire burning in the woodstove in the store. An eclectic mix of merchandise is intellectual fuel for both the curious browser and the serious shopper.

This ride starts in San Gregorio and follows inland country roads to Half Moon Bay. Rolling hills along the way keep cyclists energized as the scenery is constantly changing and car traffic is minimal. Pastureland and ranches give way to redwood forests at the *Purisima Creek Redwoods Open Space Preserve*, just before the final hill beyond which is Half Moon Bay. In Half Moon Bay, there are many shops for browsing and restaurants for food and snacks — a good place to get off the bike and unwind before heading back.

From Half Moon Bay, the route heads directly back along Highway 1. Cyclists traveling in the southern direction are usually rewarded with generous tailwinds, making the return trip to San Gregorio much shorter than the trip out.

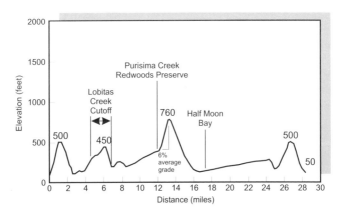

Starting Point

Start the ride in San Gregorio where there is plenty of parking. To get there, take Woodside Road (Highway 84) from Woodside up and over the hill, where it becomes La Honda Road, all the way to San Gregorio. Begin the mileage at the corner of La Honda Road and Stage Road.

Mile Markers

0.0 Proceed NORTH on Stage Road, heading out of San Gregorio.

1.1 Turn RIGHT onto Highway 1.

2.8 Cross over bridge and then turn RIGHT onto Tunitas Creek Road.

4.9 Turn LEFT onto Lobitas Creek Cutoff.

6.6 Turn RIGHT onto Verde Road.

6.7 Lobitas Creek Road intersects on the right side.

6.9 Verde Road access spur to Highway 1 on the left side.

8.5 Turn RIGHT onto Purisima Creek Road.

12.2 Purisima Creek Redwoods Preserve on the right side — begin Higgins Purisima Road at the hairpin turn.

13.2 Summit — 760 feet.

16.5 Turn RIGHT onto Main Street.

17.5 Central Half Moon Bay — return back down Main Street when you are ready.

18.5 Turn LEFT to head south on Highway 1.

25.3 Intersection with Tunitas Creek Road on the left side.

27.0 Turn LEFT onto Stage Road at the top of the hill.

28.1 End of the ride back in San Gregorio.

Pigeon Point Lighthouse

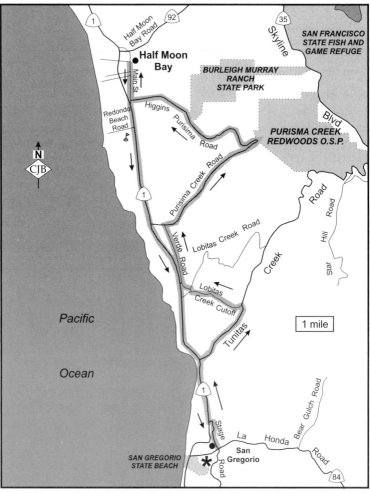

Ride No. 30

31 Loma Mar

Old Haul Road Mountain Bike

Region: *Pacific Coast*	**Distance:** *16 miles*
Difficulty Rating: *Easy*	**Elevation Gain:** *800 feet*
Skill Level: *Non-technical*	**Riding Time:** *2 hours*

About the Ride

The demand for lumber created by the California gold rush in 1849 and later by the near total destruction of San Francisco in the 1906 earthquake was met by logging the seemingly endless redwood forests of the Santa Cruz Mountains. Getting the timber out of the forests required the construction of extensive roads and railroads. One of these, no longer used for logging, is today called Old Haul Road and is located within *Pescadero Creek County Park*. It follows a route through the park from the tiny hamlet of Loma Mar, located just east of Pescadero, to *Portola State Park*. Because it was formerly used as a railroad route, the grade is generally not steep and can be negotiated easily by beginner mountain bike enthusiasts.

The route of this ride begins in Loma Mar on Highway 84 and goes through *Pescadero Creek County Park* all the way to park headquarters for *Portola State Park*, a good place to walk around and have a snack. The return is back along the same route, mostly downhill.

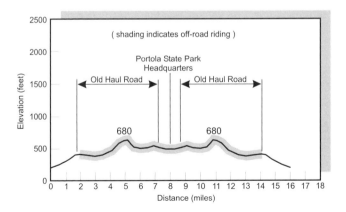

Starting Point

Start the ride in Loma Mar, about 6 miles east of Pescadero at or near the Loma Mar Store. To get there, take the Woodside Road (Highway 84) exit from Highway 280. Proceed west on Woodside Road through Woodside and over the hill toward La Honda. Just past La Honda, turn left onto Pescadero Road and follow it to Loma Mar. Park nearby and begin the mileage near the store.

Mile Markers

0.0 Proceed EAST along Pescadero Road and turn RIGHT onto Wurr Road.

1.6 Turn RIGHT into Pescadero Creek County Park on Old Haul Road and continue past the gate onto the dirt trail.

2.2 Continue past another gate.

2.4 Pomponio Trail intersection on the left side.

3.0 Towne Trail intersection on the left side.

3.5 Butano Ridge Loop Trail intersection on the right side.

5.9 Bridge Trail intersection on the left side.

6.0 Butano Ridge Loop Trail intersection on the right side.

7.1 Turn LEFT off of Old Haul Road into Portola State Park and begin a steep descent.

8.0 Portola State Park headquarters on the left side. Return back the way you came.

8.9 Turn RIGHT onto Old Haul Road, heading back toward Loma Mar.

14.4 At the end of the trail, turn RIGHT onto Wurr Road.

14.6 Turn LEFT onto Pescadero Road.

16.3 End of the ride at the Loma Mar Store.

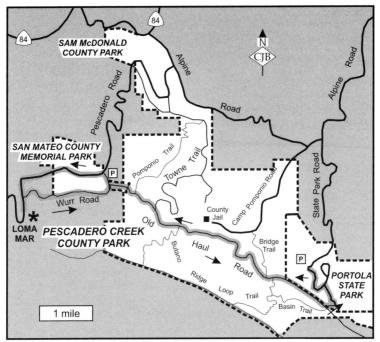

Ride No. 31

IVERSON CABIN

Courtesy of Santa Cruz Mountains Natural History Associations

32   Pescadero
Butano State Park Mountain Bike

Region: *Pacific Coast*	**Distance:** *13 miles*
Difficulty Rating: *Difficult*	**Elevation Gain:** *2000 feet*
Skill Level: *Somewhat technical*	**Riding Time:** *2-3 hours*

About the Ride

Just south of the tiny community of Pescadero lies *Butano State Park* (pronounced bū'tan-o). The name, Butano, evolved from the original name, as shown on early maps of the area, Beutno. Oddly, whereas the meaning of Beutno, in the Ohlone Indian language from which it came, was "friendly meeting place," the Spanish word, Butano, means "butane."

Somewhat isolated and difficult to get to from most Bay Area cities, *Butano State Park* has retained its charm for campers and hikers as well as mountain bike enthusiasts. Once the home of the Ohlone Indians and later, of settlers who logged the lush mountains heavily, it now is undergoing a constant recovery as the second-growth redwoods regain the majesty of their ancestors. While most trails inside the park are off-limits to bicycles, fire roads around the park periphery permit mountain bikers to experience the beauty of the mountains from the ridges above.

The route of this ride first follows along Cloverdale Road from the park entrance north about a mile to a trailhead for Butano Fire Road. The climb along the ridge is on a fairly gentle grade as the fire road gradually rises above the park valley and ultimately crosses an old landing strip. Views both to the east and to the coast in the west from the ridge top present themselves at the top of the climb. The return to the park center is along Olmo Fire Road, a route that is generally downhill but that also has some steep uphill sections along the way.

The main climb along Butano Fire Road is long but not steep. The trails are all wide and not technical. The only steep uphill sections are along the descent on Olmo Fire Road.

Starting Point

Start the ride at the entrance to *Butano State Park*. From Palo Alto, head west on Page Mill Road and follow it all the way to Skyline Boulevard at the top. Continue straight across Skyline Boulevard to get on Alpine Road and proceed toward Pescadero. Turn left on Pescadero Road at the bottom of the hill. Go over another hill and then, just before entering Pescadero, turn left onto Cloverdale Road. *Butano State Park* is on Cloverdale Road, about 4 miles distant.

To get there from Santa Cruz, go north along Highway 1. Continue for about 19 miles and then turn right onto Gazos Creek Road. Turn left onto Cloverdale Road and the park entrance is about 1 mile away.

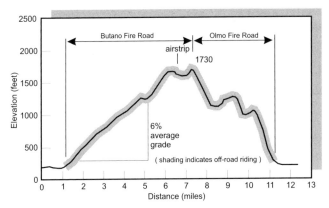

Mile Markers

0.0 Proceed NORTH along the Cloverdale Road.

0.9 Look for the fire road on the right side before you get to Canyon Road. Turn RIGHT onto the fire road — Butano Fire Road — and proceed around the gate which is usually locked.

2.5 Mill Ox Trail intersection on the right side.

3.6 Bear RIGHT at the trail split. To the left is private property.

4.1 Pass through an unused open gate.

4.3 Continue STRAIGHT on Butano Fire Road at the intersection with Jackson Flats Trail on the right side.

6.2 Continue STRAIGHT across an abandoned airstrip.

6.7 Continue STRAIGHT on Butano Fire Road at the intersection with the trail to the Butano Trail Camp on the right side.

7.1 Turn RIGHT onto Olmo Fire Road. This is EASY TO MISS. If you reach the trailhead for the Ray Linder Memorial Trail on the left side, you went too far.

8.1 Indian Trail intersection on the right side.

8.8 There is a short trail on the left side to an overlook with a bench.

9.9 Goat Hill Trail intersection on the right side.

10.4 Año Nuevo Trail intersection on the left side.

11.0 Turn LEFT onto the service road at the end of the Olmo Fire Road.

11.6 Turn LEFT on the main paved road toward the park exit.

12.4 Back at the start point.

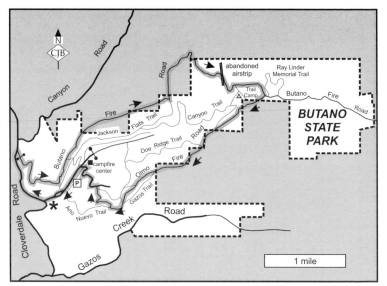

Ride No. 32

Butano State Park

APPENDIX

RIDES BY RATINGS

Memorial Church at Stanford University

BICYCLING TIPS

Familiarize yourself with these simple tips to make your self a better and safer cyclist.

GENERAL RULES OF THE ROAD

1. Always ride on the right side of the road and never against the flow of traffic. Remember that bicycles are subject to the same laws as cars.

2. Keep as far to the right as possible in order to allow cars sufficient room to pass. Always ride in single file when traffic is present.

3. Signal when you are turning or slowing down in order to allow following riders to prepare for the same and to indicate to cars what you are doing. Never act suddenly, except in an emergency.

4. Never ride on freeways except where bicycles are specifically permitted.

5. Cross railroad tracks and cattle guards perpendicularly. In wet conditions, these may be very slippery and it may be necessary to walk your bike across to ensure your safety.

6. In rain or in wet road conditions, ride slower and more cautiously then you normally would. Not only are the pavements slippery, but your brakes will not grab as well when they are wet.

7. Avoid night riding. If you absolutely must, be sure to wear bright clothing and to carry a flashing light.

8. Never assume that another car or cyclist will yield to you. Ride assertively, but be cautious and defensive.

9. Use extra care when passing parked cars. Watch for doors to open suddenly.

10. Avoid riding on sidewalks unless signs indicate that bicycles are permitted or if traffic conditions are so dangerous that you have no choice.

11. When making a left turn in traffic, ride assertively and give clear signals as to your intentions. Be courteous and show appreciation when a vehicle pauses to give you clearance.

12. Always stop at red lights and stop signs. Bicycles have no special privileges.

13. Signal the presence of road debris or potholes to cyclists following behind you.

OFF-ROAD BIKING

1. Know the rules for the area in which you are riding. Always stay on trails intended for bikes. Leave the area just as you found it.
2. Yield to equestrians. Horses may spook when a bicycle appears suddenly. When approaching from behind, talk loudly so the horse can hear you coming. Most horses are familiar with human voices, but not with bicycles.
3. Yield to hikers. It is important to share the trails harmoniously.
4. Always be courteous. Nothing is worse for the sport than hostility between trail users.
5. Look ahead to anticipate encounters. Approach blind curves slowly.
6. Avoid contact with plant life along the trails. Poison oak is very common in northern California and can be a very unpleasant experience.
7. Carry maps at all times, unless you are very familiar with the area.
8. Mountain bike tires can be deflated a small amount to provide for better traction in loose conditions.
9. Lower your saddle before you begin a steep downhill. This will give you a lower center of gravity and will reduce the chance of your being launched over the handlebars if you hit an obstacle.

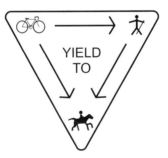

EQUIPMENT

1. Always carry a spare tube, patch kit, pump and tools.
2. Be prepared to fix your own bike if problems arise. Don't depend on others to do this for you unless you have a tacit understanding.
3. Check your equipment before you go, not after you are underway. Check for tire pressure and for proper operation of brakes and gear shifters.
4. Road riding requires fully inflated tires. Soft tires can result in punctures when sharp bumps or potholes are encountered.

5. Carry adequate amounts of water.
6. If you ride at night, make sure your bike is equipped with reflectors.
7. Toe clips or clipless pedals are much more comfortable than flat pedals, especially on long rides. They make climbing easier, too.
8. A rear view mirror is a useful accessory by permitting you to see approaching cyclists and vehicles without turning around.
9. Carry a lock when you expect to leave your bike unattended.

CLOTHING

1. A helmet is mandatory for obvious safety reasons.
2. Wear bright clothing that can be easily seen by motorists.
3. Lycra shorts offer more comfort on long rides than loose fitting shorts.
4. Gloves are not absolutely necessary, but can help you avoid blisters or blood circulation problems.
5. Carry a lightweight windbreaker if you expect to encounter changing weather conditions.
6. Wear goggles or some other form of eyewear to protect your eyes from the harmful effects of the sun and from dirt and debris that may be present.

TECHNIQUE

1. A properly adjusted seat height will ensure your comfort and will help to avoid knee injuries. The correct height will result in a slight bend in the knee when the leg is fully extended to the lower of the two pedals.
2. Be familiar with gear shifting so you can anticipate the hill climbs and shift before you need to. It is sometimes difficult to shift when you are in the middle of a steep climb. Always keep the pedals moving when you shift.
3. The upright position on dropped handlebars is usually the most comfortable position for most road riding. Position yourself on the lower part of the bars when you are going downhill to get the most leverage on the brakes.
4. When riding in a group, it is both safe and polite to regroup frequently. Avoid getting spread out over long distances.

ABOUT THE AUTHOR

Born in New Jersey, Conrad Boisvert has been a resident of northern California since 1972. With a long career as a microelectronics engineer, he has been a recreational cyclist for many years. Not only has he toured the many roads and trails in and around the Bay Area, but he has also cycled throughout the continental United States and in Hawaii, Alaska, Canada, Mexico, Costa Rica, New Zealand, Bali, Ireland, France, Italy, and Austria. He is the author of three other bicycle guidebooks and currently resides in Aptos and in the Sierras.

The author in Death Valley

THE BAY AREA BIKE TRAILS SERIES

The Bay Area Bike Trails Series offers over 185 self-guided road and mountain bicycle tours. Each ride contains clear, detailed maps, easily followed directions with mile markers, elevation profiles of the terrain, beautiful photographs, historical background and points of interest.

Bay Area Mountain Bike Trails, 2nd Edition by Conrad J. Boisvert, 2004. $18.95. The Bay Area offers some of the most exciting and scenic off-road trails and a wealth of hidden trails, all within easy access of major cities. From Santa Rosa south to Gilroy, you can ride along the spectacular ridges of Mt. Tamalpais, view the Golden Gate Bridge from the Marin Headlands, or challenge yourself on the hills of Mt. Diablo.

East Bay Bike Trails by Conrad J. Boisvert, 1992 (latest revision 2002). $15.95. Somewhat sheltered from coastal fog and ocean winds, the East Bay extends from the Carquinez Strait south to Fremont. Interesting bike routes take you through heavily wooded hills above Oakland and Berkeley, orchards and farms around Brentwood, eerie windmills in Livermore, the wetlands around Newark, and dramatic Mt. Diablo in Danville.

Marin County Bike Trails by Phyllis L. Neumann, 1989 (latest revision 2001). $15.95. Just across the Golden Gate Bridge, Marin County combines exquisite natural beauty with sophisticated elegance to give you spectacular views, rugged cliffs, natural beaches, well-developed parks, rural farmlands, tiny hidden towns and Mt. Tamalpais. A specially designed bike route from Petaluma to the Golden Gate Bridge is also included.

San Francisco Peninsula Bike Trails, 2nd Edition by Conrad J. Boisvert, 2004. $17.95. Few areas can compare with the spectacular San Francisco Peninsula, which encompasses the wooded foothills around Woodside, dense redwood forests in the Santa Cruz mountains and remote country roads along the rugged Pacific coastline.

Sonoma County Bike Trails, 3rd Edition by Phyllis L. Neumann, 1999 (latest revision 2001). $15.95. Less than an hour's drive north from San Francisco brings you to tranquil country roads, gently rolling farmlands, towering redwoods, lush vineyards, local wineries, the Russian River and the Pacific coastline. A specially designed bike route from Cloverdale to Petaluma is also included.

South Bay Bike Trails, 2nd Edition by Conrad J. Boisvert, 2000. (latest revision 2001) $15.95. Better known for its high-tech image, once you head out into the surrounding countryside, the South Bay is a cyclist's paradise. From San Jose south to Gilroy, picturesque rides take you through ranchlands around Morgan Hill, dense redwood forests in the Santa Cruz mountains, and the coastal wetlands of the Elkhorn Slough. Heading south along the Pacific coast brings you to the famous seaside resorts and beaches of Santa Cruz and Capitola.